PENGUIN BOOKS

NONALIGNMENT 2.0

Sunil Khilnani is Avantha Professor and Director of the India Institute, King's College London, and author of *The Idea of India*.

Rajiv Kumar, an economist, is Senior Fellow at the Centre for Policy Research. He was secretary general of the Federation of Indian Chambers of Commerce and Industry (FICCI), and former director of the Indian Council for Research on International Economic Relations (ICRIER).

Pratap Bhanu Mehta is President of the Centre for Policy Research, New Delhi, and a leading columnist.

Lt Gen. (Retd) Prakash Menon is Military Adviser in the National Security Council Secretariat, and was earlier commandant of the National Defence College, New Delhi.

Nandan Nilekani was co-founder and former CEO of Infosys and was chairman of the Unique Identification Authority of India (UIDAI) till March 2014.

Srinath Raghavan is Senior Fellow at the Centre for Policy Research and author of *War and Peace in Modern India: A Strategic History of the Nehru Years*, and most recently *1971: A Global History of the Creation of Bangladesh*.

Shyam Saran was foreign secretary of India and has served as the prime minister's special adviser and envoy on nuclear issues and climate change. Formerly ambassador to Nepal, Myanmar and Indonesia, he is currently Chairman of the National Security Advisory Board.

Siddharth Varadarajan is former editor of *The Hindu*, a leading commentator on foreign policy and has edited *Gujarat: The Making of a Tragedy*.

NONALIGNMENT 2.0

A FOREIGN & STRATEGIC POLICY
FOR INDIA IN THE 21ST CENTURY

SUNIL KHILNANI • RAJIV KUMAR • PRATAP BHANU MEHTA
LT GEN. (RETD) PRAKASH MENON • NANDAN NILEKANI
SRINATH RAGHAVAN • SHYAM SARAN • SIDDHARTH VARADARAJAN

WITH A NEW PREFACE

PENGUIN BOOKS

PENGUIN BOOKS

USA | Canada | UK | Ireland | Australia
New Zealand | India | South Africa | China

Penguin Books is part of the Penguin Random House group of companies
whose addresses can be found at global.penguinrandomhouse.com

Published by Penguin Random House India Pvt. Ltd
7th Floor, Infinity Tower C, DLF Cyber City,
Gurgaon 122 002, Haryana, India

Penguin
Random House
India

First published in Viking by Penguin Books India 2013
Published in Penguin Books 2014

ISBN 9780143423478

Typeset in Garamond by R. Ajith Kumar, New Delhi
Printed at Repro Knowledgecast Limited, India

www.penguin.co.in

Contents

Contents

Preface to the Paperback Edition

The paperback edition of *NonAlignment 2.0* is published at a particularly opportune time: a moment when the epochal political transition underway in India coincides with a renewed opportunity to set a coherent national agenda, one that can achieve India's transformation into a great power, based on the principles of democracy and inclusive development.

NonAlignment 2.0 is intended by its authors to generate an informed debate about the challenges India confronts, both domestic and external, as well as the considerable assets this country possesses to face those challenges. Our title, unfortunately, has proved something of a distraction—sometimes leading to more discussion than the actual substance of our arguments. While the title is of secondary importance, we believe that the substantive options set out in the book are based on analytic realism about our current predicament as well as optimism about our extraordinary potential. We remain encouraged by the lively debate the text has stimulated, and we hope that the appearance of the paperback edition will broaden that circle of debate in our country, precisely at a time when there is a sense of transformational change in the air and hope prevails about India's prospects both at home and abroad. It's a moment that demands to be seized. In the first instance, key and long-overdue reforms can now be implemented by an electorally empowered leadership. Beyond that, we also need an intellectual map to guide the pursuit of our values and interests. *NonAlignment 2.0* has identified the choices that confront India in its quest for greatness and it outlines a comprehensive national strategy which leverages the country's strengths even as it seeks to overcome its vulnerabilities.

For example, India has a potential demographic dividend in its young and growing population, but needs to provide expanding employment opportunities to reap that dividend. This, in turn, implies an ability to sustain a high rate of economic growth, in particular, accelerated growth in manufacturing, and this demands an educated and skilled work force. India's development prospects are also linked to its ability to ensure domestic peace and security while creating an external environment that is supportive of India's development and welcomes its emergence as a great power. This translates into a need for urgent governance reforms, a recognition that many of the country's internal security challenges draw their energy from long-standing economic and social grievances, that there are serious shortcomings in the justice and policing system and that the state is often seen as an instrument of oppression rather than an assurance of redressal. Bringing about change in the domestic domain will be difficult because there are powerful and entrenched interests that will need to be confronted and neutralized. But such domestic reforms are the essential first step to India achieving its external goals. The political mandate delivered to the new government gives it a rare opportunity to succeed in this regard.

There is another compelling reality requiring urgent address. Most of the challenges the world confronts today are cross-cutting and multi-sectoral in nature—they do not observe disciplinary or ministerial boundaries. This is as true in the domestic domain as it is in the external domain. For example, the challenges of ensuring water, energy and food security are integrally interlinked and require inter-disciplinary and institutionally coherent responses. Even within the domain of energy, which is a major constraint on India's ability to sustain accelerated economic growth, there is policy fragmentation with multiple agencies, often pursuing contradictory policies, involved. We must overcome our preference for compartmentalized bureaucratic structures and make inter-agency policy-making and implementation the norm rather than the exception.

The authors of *NonAlignment 2.0* have identified a strategy in the external domain that is appropriate to India's overall national objectives and transcends partisan political affiliations. To begin with, they point out that the lines of division between domestic and external are becoming increasingly blurred in today's globalized world. The external environment impacts relentlessly on domestic developments but equally, given India's size and potential, what happens in our country impacts significantly on regional and global developments. This is why there is keen interest across the world in the dramatic political change that has taken place in India. The leaders of all major countries wish to engage their counterparts in India because India's decisions will impact upon them as much as on India. India must, therefore, remain fully engaged with its external environment, constantly endeavour to shape it to serve India's interests and, above all, recognize that the ultimate test of the success or failure of India's foreign policy will lie in its contribution to the welfare of its people.

In shaping the external environment, the authors attach the highest priority to India's neighbourhood. The country cannot really aspire to a significant regional, let alone global, role, if it is unable to manage its own neighbourhood. The authors of *NonAlignment 2.0* recognize the emergence of China as the most significant challenge for India, since it is the one country which impinges directly on India's overall interests. There is a growing asymmetry between India and China but there is no reason why this asymmetry should be regarded as a permanent condition. In fact, if there is any one country that has the potential to level with China and to surpass it, it is India. If India adopts the right strategies and pursues them with consistency there is no reason why it cannot join the ranks of the world's great powers. However, India as a great power will be different from China, given its embrace of democracy and internal diversity. An economically vibrant, pluralist and democratic India has the opportunity to lead the world by the power of its example.

The China challenge requires a 'walking on two legs' strategy, which China itself has pursued over the years: namely, finding the right mix of engagement and 'constrainment'—that is, engaging with China even while being able to countervail those of its policies that impinge on our interests. This approach is likely to be maintained across changes in national government—as it needs to be. The same appears true for relations with Pakistan. *NonAlignment 2.0* recommends a series of positive and negative levers available for use to try to change the strategic calculus in Islamabad and convince Pakistan that the use of cross-border terrorism as an instrument of state policy carries huge risks for the country's own security interests.

In coming years, India is likely to be far more active and visible both on the regional and economic stage with an accent on the eastern neighbourhood, including South-East Asia and Japan. Relationships which enhance India's security and economic interests are also likely to be given priority. *NonAlignment 2.0* covers a wide spectrum of India's national security challenges: it shows their analytic integration and argues for an equally integrated policy and institutional approach to confronting these challenges.

Finally, communicating the message about India's distinctive identity and its pursuit of power will be an important instrument in shaping how the world responds to India. Indeed, as the authors argue, the need for strategic communications or the ability to anticipate and interactively respond to perceptions of domestic as well as global public opinion are essential to a national strategy.

We hope the paperback edition of this book will find

a new readership, stimulate further constructive debate across the political and party spectrum, and contribute to the challenging but essential national endeavour of navigating India to its rightful place in a transformed global landscape—a journey we now have the opportunity of pursuing with renewed energy and ambition.

June 2014

Preface to the First Edition

On 28 February 2012, 'NonAlignment 2.0' was launched as a monograph by two former national security advisers of India, Brajesh Mishra and M.K. Narayanan, and their successor in the post, Shivshankar Menon. Since its publication the monograph has generated considerable debate and even controversy. Some of the criticism was directed towards the title itself, that is, the term 'NonAlignment'. Others questioned the assessments relating to our relations with China, and still others were critical of what were seen as significant gaps in the study. For instance, attention was drawn to the absence of any separate sections on the USA, Europe or South-East Asia, despite these being important foreign policy priorities for India.

The authors have together and in their individual capacities, respectively, held several interactions with think tanks, scholars and civil society groups both in India and abroad. They felt that it would be both appropriate and timely to revise and recast the original monograph in the form of a book, incorporating some of the very useful suggestions that emerged out of these debates. They have also tried, to the best of their ability, to respond to some of the criticisms of both the format and the contents of the monograph. This book is the result of these follow-up endeavours, and the authors are thankful to Penguin India for agreeing to its early publication.

It may be worth recalling the original intent of the authors, as set out in the Preface to the earlier monograph:

> **NonAlignment 2.0** is an attempt to identify the basic principles that should guide India's foreign and strategic policy over the next decade. The views it sets out are rooted in the conviction that the success of India's own internal development will depend decisively on how effectively we manage our global opportunities in order to maximize our choices—thereby enlarging our domestic options to the benefit of all Indians.

The purposes of the present strategy document are threefold: to lay out the opportunities that India enjoys in the international sphere; to identify the challenges and threats it is likely to confront; and to define the broad perspective and approach that India should adopt as it works to enhance its strategic autonomy in global circumstances that, for some time to come, are likely to remain volatile and uncertain.

The necessity of such a document is driven by a sense of urgency among all its authors that we have a limited window of opportunity in which to seize our chances. Further, the decisions and choices we make in coming years will have long-term effects upon our future development and will set us down paths that will determine the range of subsequent future choices. It is therefore imperative that we have a clear map of the terrain which we shall have to navigate in coming years—and, equally, that we have a definite sense of the national goals, values and interests that we need to pursue with consistency and vigour.

It should be clear that the document does not intend to prescribe specific policies. Such policies remain the prerogative of government—and their definition must occur in the domain of public debate and deliberation. What our document does insist upon is the critical need for a strategic consensus and for a unified approach to India's international engagements. We believe that the principles and views set out here about our national interests should command cross-party support, as well as support from across government, the corporate community, civil society and the media. While there may be important disagreements about matters of specific policy and detail, a strategic consensus is vital if India is to be able to successfully pursue its national development goals in difficult global circumstances.

The Authors

NonAlignment 2.0 is the product of collective deliberation, debate and report writing involving a diverse and independent group of analysts and policymakers, namely, Sunil Khilnani, Rajiv Kumar, Pratap Bhanu Mehta, Lt Gen. (Retd) Prakash Menon, Nandan Nilekani, Srinath Raghavan, Shyam Saran and Siddharth Varadarajan. The group was convened in November 2010 and met at regular intervals for over a year, until January 2012. Also present at some of the meetings were the National Security Adviser Shivshankar Menon and the Deputy National Security Advisers Alok Prasad and Latha Reddy. The meetings were invariably lively and full of argument and constructive critique: the resulting text therefore should not be seen as one with whose every line all members of the group would agree. Rather than offer bland consensus, we have preferred a document that we hope will prompt further discussion and elaboration. It is the case, however, that all members of the group fully endorse the basic principles and perspectives embodied in *NonAlignment 2.0*. Indeed, we collectively wish to bring these principles to the attention of our fellow citizens and to our political leaders, policymakers and opinion shapers, in order that we might arrive at a basic national consensus about India's strategic priorities and opportunities.

Why NonAlignment 2.0?

Since the release of the monograph 'NonAlignment 2.0', several analysts and commentators have questioned the wisdom of retaining a title that is allegedly outdated and associated in public perception with a failed foreign policy. It has been pointed out that in a world that is drastically changed and still in the midst of a radical transformation, India's interests are not fully encompassed by the use of the term NonAlignment. This, it is argued, may even lead to regression in India's approach to the changing global environment.

The authors believe that the essence of NonAlignment is India's unwavering and continuing search for strategic autonomy. More specifically, it encompasses three core strategic principles that remain relevant to India's engagement with the world: the need to make independent judgements in international affairs without being unduly influenced by ideas and policies set elsewhere; the need to develop the capacity for autonomous strategic action to secure India's own interests without being excessively dependent on, or restrained by, the capabilities and interests of other powers; and the need to work towards a more equitable international order that reflects the shifting balance of aspiration and power.

In this context, it is important to distinguish between NonAlignment as a strategic doctrine underpinning India's foreign policy and the fate of the Non-Aligned Movement, which was a response to the binary geopolitics of the Cold War era. With the end of the Cold War, the Non-Aligned Movement lost its moorings though it continues to survive as a pale legacy from the past. However, nonalignment as a doctrine of India's foreign policy, and as articulated by India's first prime minister, Jawaharlal Nehru, reflected the overwhelming political consensus in newly independent India to ensure that, in a world increasingly riven by ideological and great power conflict, the country should retain its ability to take relatively autonomous decisions on issues of vital national interest.

Nonalignment did not imply passivity or sitting on the sidelines with respect to important regional and global issues of the day. India embraced an active role on the international stage, virtually since its emergence as an independent country. It mobilized the United Nations

(UN) against apartheid in South Africa, played a seminal role in the drafting of the Declaration on Human Rights, led a global movement for a nuclear weapon–free world and played a leadership role in several UN peacekeeping missions. It was the country of choice to head the International Control Commission on Laos, Cambodia and Vietnam and served on the Korean Armistice Commission. In fact, India's international profile belied its relatively modest economic and military capabilities. The contemporary narrative on nonalignment which ignores this history, and portrays India as a passive and disengaged country prior to the 1990s, is a gross distortion. Equally flawed is the assumption that nonalignment crimped India's security choices during the Cold War. On the contrary, it enabled India to craft arrangements that were more attuned to its interests than formal alliances which demanded a high degree of conformity and specialization. Nor is the strategic doctrine of nonalignment passé merely because it was conceived in an older context. After all, key components of contemporary strategic vocabulary and thought—deterrence and coercion, containment and intervention—date back to the Cold War years.

It is true that during the Cold War era, India pursued a policy of economic self-reliance, shying away from the export and foreign investment–led strategies of East and

South-East Asian economies. Despite its modest footprint in the global economy, India nevertheless played a leading role in seeking a more equitable global trade and financial system. It was and has remained a key player in the World Trade Organization (WTO). What drives India's increased influence as a major power today is the confluence of its tradition of global political engagement with more recent growing global economic engagement. NonAlignment 2.0 is an exploration of the opportunities that have been unleashed by this confluence, giving India the wherewithal to play a more active role in a rapidly transforming international terrain, where political and economic power are becoming more diffused, creating the space that India has all along sought to pursue its own destiny. It is our belief that in fact nonalignment as a strategy has become more pertinent than ever as a compass for defining India's choices and decisions—provided we are able to update and renovate some of its assumptions and arguments.

Introduction

India is at a pivotal moment in its history. The extraordinary changes of the last two decades are fundamentally transforming India's economy and society. These changes have, for the first time in history, created the possibility that India can become a reasonably prosperous and equitable society. Given its scale, a successful India is destined to leave an extraordinary footprint on the world, and define future possibilities for humankind.

The fundamental source of India's power in the world is going to be the power of its example. If India can maintain high growth rates, leverage that growth to enhance the capabilities of all its citizens, and maintain robust democratic traditions and institutions, there are few limits to its global role and influence. The foundations of India's success will therefore depend on its developmental model. If our developmental model is successful, it will give us still greater legitimacy in the world—and it will enhance our capacity to act for ourselves, in pursuit of our

3

values and interests, in the international arena. By the same token, our competitors will, from time to time, impugn the validity of our model and seek to place obstructions in its path.

This has two implications for India's future strategy. Under no circumstances should India jeopardize its own domestic economic growth, its social inclusion and its political democracy. Its approach to the outside world must be to secure the maximum space possible for its own economic growth. But this pursuit of economic growth will in turn require India to confront new challenges—challenges whose roots and dynamics often lie in a volatile global environment. We need therefore to ask: What kind of foreign and strategic policy is appropriate to India's development requirements?

Despite immense challenges, India faces a broadly propitious environment for its growth. A range of factors—demography, the unleashing of domestic entrepreneurship, the rising aspirations and innovation of millions of marginalized people, technology—give India's growth prospects a sound foundation and provide a competitive advantage that could sustain growth for some time to come. There is widespread consensus that the main thing that can hold India back is India itself. There are no alibis if we were, in these circumstances, to fail.

But while the underlying trends are propitious, time is of the essence. This is so in two senses. The window of opportunity for India to become a prosperous nation is relatively small: the basic structures and dynamics necessary to achieve this prosperity will have to be put in place in the next ten to fifteen years. The underlying factors propitious for our growth may not endure long. Further, our future possibilities are going to be heavily path-dependent. That is, once certain institutional choices and development pathways are adopted, it will be very hard to change them: they will become entrenched. So, the choices we make now will define the horizons of our possibility for decades, if not longer. It follows that rather than imagining that growth can allow us to postpone hard decisions, our strategic approach must be exactly the opposite. If we do not seize the opportunities provided by a relatively benign environment, we will not get a second chance to correct our mistakes. For instance, if India wants to avoid the 'middle income trap' that has afflicted many other societies where growth rates experienced rapid acceleration only to peter out, then it will have to move decisively and rapidly across a range of issues.

The nature of modern societies compels those who wish to be successful to do two things simultaneously. For one, successful countries need to prioritize their aims and focus their energies on those basic priorities. For another, minor deficiencies can have a major impact across the system. That the kingdom can be lost for want of a horseshoe nail is not just a nursery rhyme: it is a parable about the nature of power. A host of factors, both very large and very small, go into the making of effective power; and India does not have the option of neglecting any of them. Grand strategy and fine-grained analysis and action have to be pursued in tandem.

The core objective of a strategic approach should be to give India maximum options in its relations with the outside world—that is, to enhance India's strategic space and capacity for independent agency. This in turn will give it maximum options for its own internal development. Such an approach will preserve and sustain two core objectives of nonalignment in a changing world. This policy can therefore be described as 'NonAlignment 2.0'—a reworking for present times of the fundamental principles that have defined India's international engagements since Independence. The core objectives of nonalignment were to ensure that India did not define its national interest or approach to world politics in terms of ideologies and goals that had been set elsewhere; that India retained maximum strategic autonomy to pursue its own developmental goals; and that India worked to build national power as the

6

foundation for creating a more just and equitable global order.

The context in which India's strategy is defined by nonalignment has changed considerably, as have India's own capacities and requirements. Any national strategy needs to adapt and to assimilate these changes if it is to be credible and effective. The most fundamental change to that context is recognition of the fact that our economic growth requires deepened economic engagement with the outside world at all levels: trade, labour, technology and ideas. It is therefore central to any future Indian strategy that we strive to maintain an open global order at many different levels.

The material preconditions for our economic success have grown correspondingly complex. India now has an increasing range of interests, which are anchored in different parts of the world and which stem from a vast array of factors: for instance, the need to secure energy and other vital natural resources; the responsibility to protect the rights of Indian labour overseas; the imperative to maintain open shipping lanes; the need to seek and protect Indian investments overseas; and the need to secure trade access.

In ensuring our economic growth, one factor is even more fundamental than access to resources. This is our ability to compete in the field that is vital to defining national power in the twenty-first century: knowledge and knowledge production, especially the capacity to innovate and to generate new forms of knowledge, both pure and applied. Economic growth, if it is to be both sustainable in terms of resources and competitive across global markets, will depend ever more completely on scientific and technological progress, on developing human capital and on disseminating skills and expertise across the working citizenry. Given our scale, this will necessitate the revitalization and expansion of India's research and educational infrastructure, right from the apex pure research institutes down to the access points for effectively imparting primary education and vocational skills to the wider citizenry.

The complexity of India's material interests and their intermeshing with the imperatives of human capital formation and knowledge production have profound implications for how we think of foreign and strategic policy. For one thing, it will make it much more difficult for us to adopt stances rooted in abstract idealism, or to seek to follow a narrow analysis of what serves our national interest. The complexity of our national interests, given both the material and intellectual dimensions which define them, makes articulating a coherent, effective national strategy a far more subtle task than any simply specified pursuit of power. We will need to develop a strategic culture—rooted in policy analysis, evaluation and research, and modes of constructive intellectual debate about our strategic options—that is attuned to this complexity.

Grasping this complexity will require, for instance, a more nuanced understanding of a whole range of concepts and principles that have guided our foreign policy: the principle of state sovereignty, the conditions under which we deploy force overseas, our approach to international negotiations in domains ranging from trade to climate change, to cite just a few examples. Our global engagement on each issue will resemble not so much a boxing match—where victory and defeat can be rapidly judged in terms of decisive punches or counterpunches—as it will a chess grandmasters' tournament, where each move will have to be mindful of several other pieces on the board and each game is played as part of a long strategic interaction.

If the complexity of material interests and the imperatives of being a knowledge-producing society preclude simple narratives, so too does the changing nature of global power. NonAlignment 2.0 has to be articulated in a context where power itself is becoming far more complex, diffused and fragmented—less a once-and-for-all achievement and more a constant wary effort to stay a few moves ahead of competitors and opponents.

In contrast to the twentieth century, the twenty-first century is unlikely to be characterized by a world bifurcated between two dominant powers. While China and the United States will undoubtedly remain superpowers, it is unlikely that they will be able to exercise the kind of consistent, full-spectrum global dominance that superpowers exercised during the mid-twentieth-century Cold War. Alongside the US and China, there will be several other centres and hubs of power that will be relevant, particularly in regional contexts. This means that nonalignment will no longer be limited to avoiding becoming a front-line state in a conflict between two powers. It will instead require a very skilful management of complicated coalitions and opportunities—in environments that may inherently be unstable and volatile rather than structurally settled. It is this very openness and fluidity that has the potential to provide India with rich opportunities, especially if it can leverage into the international domain some of its domestically acquired skills in coalition management and complex interest negotiation.

India will also inhabit an economic world where the other great binary of the twentieth century, the polarity between the developed and the developing world, is undergoing substantial redefinition. India's interests, as those of many countries, will straddle this divide, and be heterogeneous in character. As in global geopolitics, it is unlikely that there will be enduring coalitions based on fixed structural positions on one or the other side of this divide in the world economy. Coalitions will be a lot more contingent and fluid, and will need artful management.

One of the great lessons of the late twentieth century centred on the destabilizing effects of asymmetries in power. The capacity of even small powers or non-state groups to generate effects disproportionate to their physical scale or their ostensible material power has become evident. In an age when technology can place weapons of great potency in the hand of non-sovereign agencies and otherwise weak states, and when new media forms can diffuse information and images that can delegitimize national reputations, the apparently less powerful can produce massive impacts and effects on more powerful states, and can thereby transform horizons and options. Therefore the kinds of power that a state requires will take two different forms. On the one hand, the fact remains that great power competition of a classical kind will continue to define aspects of the global order. We must seek therefore to ensure that no other state is in a position to exercise undue influence on us—or make us act against our better judgement and will. On the other hand, we need to devise appropriate responses that address the unpredictable ways in which weak states, terrorist groups and new postmodern Internet- and media-based and other forms of power can influence or threaten our interests. Our institutions, our technologies, our resources and our knowledge and analytic capacities will have to undergo radical shifts and enhancements if they are to respond to both types of extant power, and to their new configurations.

India's great advantage is that, barring certain perceptions in our immediate neighbourhood, it is not seen as a threatening power. The overseas projection of Indian power has been very limited; in its external face, India's nationalism does not appear belligerently to any country, nor as expansionist or threatening in any way. This has, in some respects, been a great asset to India. Its power has often been the power of its example. The world recognizes that it needs India to succeed. This is an asset that we have rather taken for granted, and it behoves us now to leverage that global consensus as effectively as we can.

By the same token, however, India is at times perceived as a power that, even when its interests are adversely affected, can do no harm; that it is overly passive. In a range of relationships and contexts, India's ability to retaliate is seen as limited. Here, our big challenge will be at once to develop a repertoire of instruments to signal—and where necessary to establish—that there will be serious costs to attempts to coerce Indian judgements or actions, while at the same time ensuring that we do not appear threatening to our many friends and well-wishers.

While the nature of global power is undergoing redefinition and thereby enjoins states to generate new capabilities to acquire and sustain such power, it is also the case that domestic political authority and legitimacy will have to be maintained in more competitive and stringent conditions. This is because new forms of citizen mobilization and vigilance are coming to prevail, particularly in democratic societies. In this regard, effective state security will above all be a function of state openness. Accountability, adherence to norms and a capacity to enable pluralism to flourish, all will be essential to enabling states to command domestic legitimacy, and thus also to possess global credibility. Such state legitimacy will also depend on state capacity: on the state being able to effectively deliver public goods and services, and to discharge its law and security responsibilities. Enhancing state capacity in all respects must therefore be recognized as a basic element of India's strategic conception.

CHAPTER 1

The Asian Theatre

India has a long history of political, cultural and economic influence radiating across a vast expanse of contiguous land and oceanic space. Towards the west, its footprint ranged across West Asia and along the eastern coast of Africa. Towards the east, the imprint of India may be found in South-East Asia, China and as far as Japan. Central Asia is the third corner of this triangle, where ancient trade caravans from and to India carried Indian goods, religious thought, culture and ideas, whose traces remain prominent till today. It should come as no surprise therefore that as India's global imprint expands in the contemporary era, these regions of historical interaction gain prominence in India's engagement with the outside world. One of the first diplomatic initiatives of independent India's leaders was to convene the Asian Relations Conference in New Delhi in 1947, followed by the Afro-Asian Conference in Bandung in 1955. The Asian resurgence that Jawaharlal Nehru passionately believed in and championed has now become a reality. The Asian theatre has emerged as one of the key components of India's foreign and strategic policy.

In recent times, the economies of Asia have displayed extraordinary dynamism. Asian markets will be important for India; Indian markets in turn will be important for other Asian economies. Asia is likely to remain a significant source of investment in India. Intensifying economic engagement with Asia, at all levels of economic activity, will remain vital for India's interests. India's Look East Policy and its pursuit of free trade agreements (FTAs) in Asia are important steps in this direction. India must look upon Asia as the principal zone of economic opportunity.

Asia is also likely to be a theatre where a range of new institutional innovations take root. These institutions will seek to regulate and coordinate both economic activity and political relationships in Asia. They will necessarily have a variable geometry in terms of their composition, purpose and scope. Much of the competition for influence will be played out on the terrain of access and who gets membership in which institutions. Some institutions like a potential Asian monetary fund will be economic; others like the East Asian Summit will also have strategic and political importance. It is in India's interest to remain engaged with these institutions in their variety with full diplomatic attention.

Asia is also likely to be the theatre of many strategic rivalries. Asia has several outstanding territorial disputes, many of which involve China. While these disputes have, for the most part, been managed for several decades, they now have the potential to become flashpoints for military assertion and conflict in areas ranging from Taiwan and the South China Sea to India's own borders. China's economic and strategic footprint in Asia is enormous. At the same time, many Asian powers are looking to hedge their bets against excessive dependence on a major power. There is considerable interest in the United States to retain a significant role in Asia—and the United States is itself reweighting its Asian presence. The shifting contours of the Sino-US competition in Asia will need analytic and practical vigilance. Many countries are also looking to India to assume a more active strategic and economic role in Asia. So far, India has not often fully responded to the opportunities provided by the hedging strategies of various Asian powers.

Asia, with its vast oceans, its dynamic economies and its diverse political formations, is also likely to be the theatre of intense maritime competition. This is an area of serious concern, but also potentially of comparative advantage for India. India's maritime strategy, if pursued with vigour, could give it considerable strategic advantage in Asia.

Finally, Asia is likely to be a theatre of competition in ideological hegemony as well. It is a region with a wide range of successful developmental models, jostling for supremacy. It is a region with enormous cultural vitality and flows of ideas and people. And it is also a region where battles over democracy, rights and the rule of law are likely to continue. India will gain enormously by an enhanced cultural and ideational engagement with the rest of Asia. If there is to be a common Asian century, the flow of ideas from India will be vital to it. We need to invest intellectual capital in Asia.

China

China will, for the foreseeable future, remain a significant foreign policy and security challenge for India. It is the one major power which impinges directly on India's geopolitical space. As its economic and military capabilities expand, its power differential with India is likely to widen further. China has just undergone a major leadership transition. It is still unclear in what direction the new leaders will steer their country and whether there will be any significant impact on India–China relations.

As is well known, India and China have long-standing disagreements on an agreeable border. Skirmishes and incidents have occurred across the Line of Actual Control. Our strategy should be to 'hold the line' in the north on the Sino-Indian land frontier, but maintain and, if possible, enlarge India's current edge in the maritime south. This strategy takes into account both the superiority of current Chinese deployments and posture on the land boundary and the unlikelihood of the border issue being resolved in the near future.

Given that China has managed to settle many of its border issues (at least for the time being) with other, smaller neighbours, the dispute on the Indian border stands out quite prominently. While we should press for an early and satisfactory settlement to the border issue, and should welcome any positive Chinese steps in this direction that the new leadership there may offer, we need also to be prepared for the matter remaining unresolved for some time to come. It is important that we accelerate the upgradation of our border infrastructure (especially in terms of habitation and supply lines) to reduce the asymmetry in our capabilities and deployments. At the same time we must put in place operational concepts and capabilities to deter any significant incursions from the Chinese side (these are dealt with in Chapter Three).

Currently India has the edge in terms of maritime capabilities but China is catching up rapidly. China's current focus is on acquiring dominance in the Yellow Sea, the Taiwan Straits, the East China Sea and the South China Sea. The Indian Ocean falls second in the present order of priority. It is in our interest that China remains preoccupied with its first-tier, more immediate maritime theatre. The retention of strong US maritime deployments in the Asia-Pacific theatre, a more proactive and assertive Japanese naval force projection and a build-up of the naval capabilities of such key littoral states as Indonesia, Australia and Vietnam, all may help delay, if not deter, the projection of Chinese naval power in the Indian Ocean. We need to use this window of opportunity to build up our own naval capabilities. Our regional diplomacy should support this approach by fostering closer relations with these 'countervailing' powers. This should include a network of security cooperation agreements with these states and regular naval exercises with them.

On the political side, our posture towards China must be carefully nuanced and constantly calibrated in response to changing global and regional developments. China's threat perception vis-à-vis India has both a local and a global dimension. The local dimension involves Tibet. Our Tibet policy needs to be reassessed and readjusted. Persuading China to seek reconciliation with the Dalai Lama and the exiled Tibetan community may contribute to easing India–China tensions. The initial soundings must be discreet and exploratory. And we must be mindful of the risk of hostile reaction, particularly from conservative sections of the People's Liberation Army. The situation vis-à-vis Tibet has been complicated by the transition to a democratically elected Tibetan government-in-exile. The Chinese had, in part, expected that the Tibetan community would continue with its traditional method of selecting the Dalai Lama—a method that was amenable to manipulation by China. The Dalai Lama's popular legitimacy among his own people is a fact that the Chinese government must acknowledge.

On the global canvas, China looks upon India not as a threat in itself, but as a 'swing state' whose association with potential adversaries could constrain China. The challenge for Indian diplomacy will be to develop a diversified network of relations with several major powers to compel China to exercise restraint in its dealings with India, while simultaneously avoiding relationships that go beyond conveying a certain threat threshold in Chinese perceptions. This will require a particularly nuanced handling and coordination of our foreign policy, both through diplomatic and military channels. If China perceives India as irrevocably committed to an anti-China containment ring, it may end up adopting overtly hostile and negative policies towards India, rather than making an effort to keep India on a more independent path.

India–China economic relations also present a complex and somewhat ambiguous picture. Bilateral trade is rising rapidly but asymmetrically, with a growing trade surplus in favour of China. We could respond by trying to limit Chinese penetration of our market, particularly our infrastructure market. Or, we could allow access but with various conditions that safeguard and promote Indian interests in other areas. Given that India's infrastructure market is likely to be in the region of a trillion dollars in the next few years, China would obviously have a keen interest in expanding access to it. We should see this Chinese economic interest as a point of leverage for trade-offs favourable to us in other sectors, including political concessions in areas of interest to India.

One of the big concerns in our economic relations is the involvement of China's state-owned and -supported enterprises. Chinese banks are often able to offer preferential financing to Chinese companies because of their scale and because they are not driven solely by market forces. Many of China's premier manufacturing firms are also state-run, and thus have access to such financing. This means that when Chinese companies participate in competitive bidding for open tenders, they may actually have a big advantage over other bidders, which allows them to place stronger (lower) bids. However, such preferential financing could also be a useful asset in terms of the volume of infrastructure financing, so we need to develop systematic and differentiated approaches to the various issues at stake, which can balance immediate requirements with the longer-term implications of certain choices. There is the additional problem of the potential for espionage and intelligence gathering through software means, which was evidenced by the banning of import of Chinese telecom equipment.

Given the asymmetry in the economic and trade relationship, we should not overestimate our bargaining power. It may be more realistic to link large orders to economic and trade concessions, including fixed investments in India-based facilities. It is also reasonable to expect that growing economic interdependence might help make the political relationship more manageable and less subject to oscillations (though we should also bear in mind Japan's less than positive experience with China in this respect).

The growing trade surplus between India and China has been a cause for concern owing both to its degree and composition. Not only is the degree of dependence of Indian industries on Chinese imports on the rise, but

India's main exports to China are in the form of natural resources, whereas its imports are largely higher-end manufactured goods. Given India's large services sector, it should be pushing for greater market access and presence in China to correct this imbalance.

One area where India may be able to bargain effectively with China is the domain of technology transfer. The ability to leverage access to our markets in order to secure access to sophisticated technology, and so to develop domestic capacity, is something India has not been able to do as effectively as it must, especially with developed countries. By way of example, when an airline company like Indigo signs a $16 billion deal with Airbus, technology transfer should be a part of the terms of negotiation. Even India's defence offsets have been quite disappointing in terms of technology transfer, with only the lowest value addition activities being sourced domestically.

China has managed to deal with these issues quite well, mainly because the government is able to coordinate the actions of various companies (many of which are state owned)—a luxury India does not have. It may in fact be easier to negotiate technology transfer deals with China itself than with other developed countries, which are intensely possessive about their intellectual property. China's Huawei telecom company has recently agreed to set up a research facility in Bangalore to ensure that none of its imported devices contain any kind of covert listening technologies.

India's China strategy has to strike a careful balance between cooperation and competition, economic and political interests, bilateral and regional contexts. Given the current and future asymmetries in capabilities and influence between India and China, it is imperative that we get this balance right. This is perhaps the single most important challenge for Indian strategy in the years ahead.

South Asia

Within the Asian theatre no region is more vital for India than South Asia. India cannot hope to arrive as a great power if it is unable to manage relationships within the subcontinent. South Asia is holding India back at many levels. India has to expend enormous resources managing a conflict-ridden neighbourhood. Interstate politics in South Asia has direct spillover effects into domestic and regional politics in India. India's ability to command respect is considerably diminished by the resistance it meets in the region. South Asia also places fetters on India's global ambitions. Our approaches to international law and international norms are sometimes overly inhibited by anxieties about the potential implications that our commitment to certain global norms may have for our options in the neighbourhood. Overall, the opportunity costs of this unhappy regional situation are immense for both India and the region's other states.

South Asia is home to the largest number of poor people in the world. This poverty has complex causes, but in a region where natural geography and cultural–historical linkages could provide great advantages, the political factors that have kept South Asia one of the least economically integrated regions in the world are an immense obstacle to its economic development. One of India's top strategic and foreign policy priorities must be to deepen economic engagement in South Asia.

India is the major power in the region. But this is of ambivalent strategic value. On the one hand, it is the economic dynamo that has the potential to drive better economic performance and social development across the region. On the other hand, we cannot neglect the fact that the history of interstate relations in South Asia is such that India's neighbours fear it or chafe at its perceived condescension. The reality of these perceptions matters less than the strategic challenge they present. At the very least, they make it more difficult for all our neighbours to act on policies of mutual economic benefit. The prospects of regional integration will depend not merely on a cold calculus of material interests but on whether countries in the region can reach a state of maturity and self-confidence—where they do not need a fearsome 'Other' to secure their sense of self and identity. South Asia is a strategic challenge because its problems lie as much in the realm of collective moral psychology as that of conventional strategy.

Meeting this challenge will require sensitivity and agility on India's part. First, India will have to be willing to go the extra mile to reassure its neighbours, particularly the smaller ones. India has to safeguard its vital interests, and must recognize that its neighbours also have an interest in playing up the India threat to extract as many concessions as possible. This makes the task of crafting a South Asian strategy more challenging. For India will also have to be prepared for many more unilateral concessions on trade, investment and aid. Rather than insist on reciprocity or short-term equivalence, we will need to focus on longer-term goals. Building on some of its recent initiatives in this direction, India will have to single-mindedly pursue conditions that can make regional economic integration—via trade, investment, movement of people—a reality. This is a basic imperative of our regional strategy.

This situation has been further complicated by the fact

that South Asia is a region where other great powers, particularly China, are trying to expand their influence. An adequate counter-strategy will require clarity on three issues. First, we must have a much clearer assessment of which forms of Chinese engagement in the region present a threat, and which actually present an opportunity or at least converge with our own regional interests. Second, we must recognize that strategic advantage is a consequence of what we do, not what we say. The only way to counter Chinese economic engagement is to have a credible engagement plan of our own. But most important, India has lagged behind because of its inability to deliver on its promises—whether on aid or border infrastructure.

South Asia is important also for the development of India's own domestic regions. Areas like the North-East, which have remained outside the mainstream of national development, and whose people have often felt isolated, urgently require integration into the wider South Asian and Asian flows of goods and services which are bringing benefits to other parts of the region. For such parts of the country, South Asian economic integration is a necessary, not an optional, condition for growth. Different regions of India have vital stakes in our neighbours (Bengal in Bangladesh; Bihar in Nepal; Punjab in Pakistan; Tamil Nadu in Sri Lanka). We need to develop national-level policy protocols that can engage with India's regional political pressures and opportunities and leverage them to effect change in both Delhi and our neighbours.

In addition to its evident economic interdependencies, South Asia's environmental destiny is also deeply tied together. The future of our glacial systems, rivers, rainfall patterns, forest cover and wildlife hangs and falls together. It could be argued that the biggest challenge for relations in South Asia will be managing the region's environment and natural resources. Environmental risks pose clear and present threats. But they may also provide opportunities for new strategic alignments. India therefore needs to give these issues strategic priority.

Environmental challenges within the region will be both a strategic opportunity and a threat. Several treaties with Pakistan and Bangladesh serve as exemplars of how fraught river water sharing issues can be made manageable. But ecological changes are likely to ensure that disputes over matters such as water resource distribution will raise future challenges. Further, both India and Bangladesh are lower riparian states vis-à-vis China. India will now have to deploy a range of instruments to ensure its interests as a lower riparian state. All countries of the region will also have common interests in Himalayan ecology, and the implications of climate change. These common challenges do provide an opportunity to come together towards a compatible approach.

Greater regional integration will be constrained unless there is some ideological convergence on basic political values in the region. Creating opportunities to articulate cultural commonalities through cultural flows is important. Here, India needs greater commitment to encourage and enable movement of people. But in South Asia talk of cultural commonality is often perceived as reflecting an assimilationist agenda. It may therefore be more appropriate to highlight the collective commitment of all states in the region to values such as the pacification of violence, human rights, minority rights, democracy and free trade. Again, while strides have been made in these areas over the last few years, the ideological task of creating genuine intra-regional societal consensus on these values remains.

These challenges notwithstanding, India has to recognize the range of strategic opportunities it has available to it in the region. To grasp these opportunities, India will need to persuade its neighbours that its growth can be the dynamo driving forward the entire region. Second, India should also make clear that its own engagement with Asia more broadly will help to put South Asia in a larger context: that India is the region's best portal and platform to globalization. It can signal that the world is opening up to India's potential, and South Asia stays away from it at its own peril.

Pakistan

The core strategic challenge in dealing with Pakistan is simultaneously to work towards achieving a degree of normality in our relationship and to cope with present and potential threats posed by Pakistan. Thus far, the difficulty of achieving a balance between these requirements has meant that India's approach to Pakistan has periodically swung between the extremes of comprehensive engagement and almost total disengagement. India's effort to link diplomatic engagement with Pakistan to the latter's actions against terrorism has yielded diminishing returns. Breaking out of this pattern of engagement will require a range of mid-level options involving the use of positive and negative levers.

The Pakistani establishment—including the army, the ISI and the bureaucratic and political elites—believes that it is only cross-border terrorism that compels India to engage with Pakistan and accommodate its interests. On the other hand, the presence of nuclear weapons on both sides has convinced Pakistan that India will prove reluctant to initiate retaliatory responses to terrorist attacks, fearing escalation—and that this constrains any countervailing Indian strategy.

There may be differences of emphasis, but there is no fundamental gap in the perception and attitudes among different sections of the Pakistani elite. Any significant improvement in India–Pakistan relations will therefore be slow and incremental. A grand reconciliation, if at all achievable, is likely to be the cumulative culmination of incremental steps, involving shifts in establishment attitudes there—not a one-swoop decisive historic breakthrough.

While American, and more generally international, support is welcome in keeping pressure on Pakistan, we cannot depend on it to dissuade Pakistan from pursuing what it regards as a time-tested and successful foreign policy tool. As long as Pakistan is seen as delivering, even if half-heartedly, on US concerns over Al Qaeda and the Taliban in Afghanistan, only lip service will be paid to Pakistan's obligations to deliver on its promises to prevent cross-border terrorism against India. We should, of course, use the US handle as much as we can to keep up strong pressure on Pakistan. But we should recognize that this is of limited value in persuading Pakistan to abandon its use of cross-border terrorism as an instrument of state policy.

Pakistan's 'all-weather friendship' with China shields it against adverse international fallout from the pursuit of its anti-India policies. A China which is raising its regional and global profile will provide a more effective shield to Pakistan. To be sure, China does have its own concerns about the threat posed by the spread of jihadi fundamentalism in Pakistan. China may express its annoyance to Pakistan and even share its concerns with India. But Pakistan has always been quick to deliver on China's concerns and demands. It is over-optimistic to assume that we can cooperate with China in 'stabilizing' Pakistan or in dealing with the jihadi threat emanating from it. If anything, as American presence in Afghanistan ebbs and as the Pakistan Army's ability to assert control over its territory diminishes, we are likely to see an increasing Chinese role in Pakistan. In consequence, we may need to think of Pakistan as a subset of the larger strategic challenges posed by China. We should certainly engage China on this, because it is able to exert some pressure on Pakistan. But we should recognize that this is of tactical value and of limited utility.

The internal stability of Pakistan—whether it continues in the current unstable equilibrium or moves towards greater stability or instability—will be primarily determined by forces at work within Pakistan itself. There is little that India can do either to accelerate or impede a potential implosion of Pakistan. Concerns on this account must not inhibit our strategy towards Pakistan.

The aim of our Pakistan strategy must be to impart stability to our relationship. This comes down to the pursuit of two broad objectives. First, we need to ensure that no serious terrorist attacks—defined as attacks that could have significant domestic impact—are launched on Indian territory by groups based in Pakistan. Second, we need to create a situation where both sides have sufficient confidence and trust to tackle the more deep-seated and thorny outstanding disputes. Working towards these will require creating and wielding a set of negative and positive levers.

Negative Levers

The negative levers will aim to convince Pakistan that the pursuit of cross-border terrorism will not only fail to advance its objectives vis-à-vis India but also impose significant costs and risks to Pakistan's vital interests as perceived by its own elite. The former will require a robust strategy of denial. We need to make it extremely difficult for any serious terrorist attack to be pulled off on Indian soil. Doing so would mainly require strengthening our police, intelligence and counterterrorism capabilities. Over time, the growing inability of jihadi outfits to carry out such attacks is likely to reduce their attraction and utility to the Pakistan establishment.

We should also be prepared—in the event of a major terrorist attack—to convey a political signal to the Pakistan Army. The idea would be to instil a measure of caution and make them think hard before allowing another attack in the future. We have, in the past, resorted to controlled application of force across the Line of Control. Going forward, we need to move away from the notion of capturing and holding territory (however limited) to conducting effective stand-off punitive operations. (This is discussed further in Chapter Three.) Given that concerns about escalation cannot be wished away, we also need to develop other capabilities to impose behaviour-altering costs on Pakistan.

Equally, on the political front we need to develop the ability to put Pakistan diplomatically on the back foot. We should not hesitate to point out Pakistan's internal vulnerabilities. To begin with, we could express public concern over the situation in places like Balochistan and condemn human rights violations there. The level of our response could be gradually and progressively elevated. Our stance will fall well short of action on the ground, but it will gradually provide an effective tool to counter Pakistan's public posturing on Jammu and Kashmir.

Similarly, we need to gradually turn the spotlight on Pakistan-occupied Kashmir, Gilgit and Baltistan. Our quest for a Line of Control (LoC)–based solution for Jammu and Kashmir has led to the progressive neglect of our claims on these areas. This now works to our disadvantage because the LoC is seen as the starting point and an eventual compromise is envisioned in terms of an LoC-plus solution. Reasserting our claims and concerns will not only be a sensible declaratory posture, it will also help counter Pakistan's claims about Jammu and Kashmir being the 'core concern'. We should formulate and execute a media plan which puts the problems in these areas continuously in the focus, and place the issue on the agenda of India–Pakistan talks.

Our presence in Afghanistan is perceived in a negative light by Pakistan. In fact, we could build on this perception. While expressing our willingness to work with Pakistan in the stability and reconstruction of Afghanistan, we should consistently reject any special role for Pakistan in Afghanistan and make it clear that India will work with other partners to prevent the subversion of the government of Afghanistan by Pakistan or its proxies. The evolving situation in Afghanistan, especially after the withdrawal of the Western powers, will pose certain kinds of challenges for the Pakistan Army. In the short run, they may be in a stronger position because of their ability to facilitate talks with some insurgent groups. But in the long run, a diminished American presence and interest in Afghanistan will make it difficult for the Pakistan Army to extract rents from the United States. In such a situation, its interest in preserving its position and resources is likely to increase. This, in turn, may provide us with additional levers to influence its behaviour.

Positive Levers

The positive levers will aim at once to create incentives for Pakistan to respond to India's concerns and to prepare the ground for an eventual normalization of relations with Pakistan. These levers will have to be used in conjunction with the negative levers outlined above.

Our policy of making a comprehensive dialogue conditional upon Pakistan's action against terrorism has not yielded the desired results. It only provides Pakistan more opportunity to grandstand. Besides, it invests the idea of a comprehensive dialogue with needless symbolism. Indeed, we should work to reduce the symbolic significance of the mere fact of conversation and present it as no more than normal diplomacy.

Instead of breaking off talks in the event of a major provocation, we should declare that we favour continuation of the dialogue. Our position should be that it is necessary to maintain channels of communication with Pakistan at all levels to ensure that misperceptions and misunderstandings are avoided, and to enable us to convey our redlines without ambiguity. But we should leave Pakistan in no doubt that the actual pace of negotiations would be contingent on its behaviour. Our willingness to engage in discussions will have the added advantage of forestalling external interest and involvement in India–Pakistan relations. This format of engagement may be best used in conjunction with backchannel negotiations and with direct engagement with the Pakistan Army. We could then have multiple tracks and options that could be modulated in keeping with the circumstances.

We should press for military-to-military exchanges even if there is resistance on the Pakistani side. These could include proposals for sporting exchanges, military educational exchanges, invitations to military exercises, among others. If even some of these succeed, we could open up a regular exchange of personnel and views. This may not only come handy in the event of a crisis, but may also help dilute the hostile mindset.

We also need to adopt policies that will work towards the creation of constituencies in Pakistan that have a stake in peaceful and friendly relations with India. This is admittedly a long-term objective, but we should begin to lay the foundations now. We should start by promoting bilateral trade with Pakistan, by offering greater access to our market. We should keep pushing for enhanced trade relationships. Although Pakistan seems open to granting most favoured nation (MFN) status to India we cannot take it as a foregone conclusion. India should be actively pushing for a far larger volume of overland trade through the Wagah and other border points, where we could install modern inspection equipment to prevent security lapses, and facilitate two-way trade while minimizing national security concerns. We should also examine whether our developing financial sector could service some of Pakistan's business and investment requirements. India can also be a source of finance for Pakistan, thereby binding their economy into our own.

We should take the initiative on two pressing issues confronting the people of Pakistan: shortages of energy and water. We should look seriously at regional energy projects involving Pakistan, Iran, Afghanistan and Central

Asia. We should also propose discussion with Pakistan on integrated watershed management and best practices in the use and distribution of water.

The greater the exposure of ordinary Pakistanis to India, the less effective will be the official policy of deliberately cultivating a hostile attitude towards India. The promotion of exchanges at all levels among civil society, scholars, artists and students will provide a strong positive leverage for India. We can adopt unilateral measures to promote cross-border movement of people, even if there is no reciprocity. A more liberal visa regime, removing the restriction on the number of places to be visited, dispensing with the requirement of police reporting, issuing multiple-entry visas for known benign forces, especially those in the media, all these could be done unilaterally even if Pakistan does not respond. Importantly, these practices should not be interrupted in the event of rise in tensions.

The measures outlined above constitute a strategic toolbox with mid-range, positive and negative levers to influence the behaviour of Pakistan in the desired direction. The combinations in which these are wielded will depend on the evolving situation. But these capabilities and stances will provide the political leadership with a broader range of options than hitherto employed.

The current situation in Pakistan underlines the importance of preparing ourselves for certain contingencies. While a number of these could be envisioned, two situations need close attention. The first pertains to the possibility of nuclear terrorism emanating from Pakistan. This is discussed in the section on nuclear security in Chapter Five.

The second contingency that we need to prepare for is the possibility of spiralling instability in Pakistan (through political and civil conflict, or even a major environmental disaster), leading to a humanitarian crisis at our doorstep. Is it possible for us to seal our borders? If not, how do we expect to cope with a potentially large influx of Pakistanis? What lines of communication do we need to have in place to be able to work with those in Pakistan who might attempt to control this situation? These questions and more will need to be thought through well in advance. While we need to keep a close eye on the current unstable equilibrium in Pakistan we need also to develop operational contingency plans if the situation should unravel. We should not assume that all forms of instability are bad from our perspective. The challenge for our strategy is to cope with the consequences of its tipping over into outright instability.

The most important thing is that the relationship

with Pakistan should be seen in all its complexities. We should keep in mind the long-term goal of restoring the strategic unity of the subcontinent in a way compatible with the well-being of all the peoples of South Asia. A simple-minded approach that focuses only on a limited set of instruments, or is held hostage to narrow political considerations, will whittle down our strategic options and constrain our future horizons.

West Asia

In few parts of the world, outside its immediate periphery, does India have greater interests at stake than in West Asia. The region accounts for 63 per cent of our crude imports, $93 billion of trade and provides employment to 6 million Indian expatriate workers who remit over $35 billion every year. Securing and advancing these diverse sets of interests has become a pressing challenge in the wake of the political turmoil in West Asia and the contiguous parts of North Africa. This situation is likely to persist in the near to mid-term future, with unpredictable consequences for the region as a whole. While our policy towards each country will be determined by its particularities and by the evolving situation, it is important to consider these in an overarching strategic framework. In thinking about such

44

a framework, we need to bear in mind four factors that are likely to remain in play for some time in West Asia.

First, the political landscape of the region has been dramatically transformed and there is no possibility of reverting to the erstwhile status quo. Popular movements comprising new or re-energized forces powered by new forms of social communication and mobilization are now an ineradicable feature of the West Asian political terrain. These popular uprisings will throw up forces, especially Islamist political parties, which have hitherto been suppressed or marginalized by several regimes in the region. The extent to which these states' bureaucracies, military and intelligence services will be prepared and able to work with these parties remains an open question. While the elected Islamist parties might not be overtly suppressed, they are unlikely to be fully acceptable either. This will remain a key source of instability across West Asia.

Second, the strategic consequences of the US war in Iraq will continue to play out in the years ahead. It is now clear that the principal beneficiary of the war was Iran. Not only has the war resulted in the emergence of a Shiite Iraq, but it has also extended Iranian influence in Syria, Lebanon and Gaza. A corollary to this has been the Iranian drive to acquire nuclear weapons—a desire that has almost certainly been accentuated by the Western intervention in Libya. The confluence of these trends has created a sharp geopolitical divide between Iran and Saudi Arabia, and their respective allies and clients. The resulting spiral of insecurity and armament will be a principal source of tension in West Asia in the years ahead. This dynamic will play out against the backdrop of existing problems: above all Palestine, which will remain a driver of conflict in the region. The interaction of these two axes of tension will result in a more unstable regional environment.

Third, the nature of Western interests in the region is undergoing an important shift. With increasing access to other forms of energy (particularly gas) and accompanying breakthroughs in technology and marketability, Western dependence on oil from the region will certainly decline in the years ahead. However, the geopolitical importance of the region will remain undiminished—not least because of its centrality to the economies of the emerging powers. As a consequence, the United States and its allies will have greater room for manoeuvre in West Asia.

Fourth, the combination of these three factors implies that the Western propensity for intervention in the region is likely to persist despite the thinning out of Western forces on the ground. West Asia may well become the main arena for introducing and testing new norms of great power intervention. Such intervention is likely to be justified on humanitarian grounds, though these principles will continue to be applied rather selectively. One can already see this happening in Syria.

These four factors underscore certain strategic principles that need to frame our policies in West Asia. For a start, we need to engage more widely in the region than we have done so far and to build our capacity for such wide-ranging engagement. We need to be in a position to anticipate and shape developments rather than merely reacting to them. Indeed, certain types of reactive responses—evacuation of expatriate Indians during crises, for instance—will become difficult in the climate of uncertainty that lies ahead.

In particular, we need to carefully distinguish between the emerging Islamist political forces and jihadi terrorist organizations like Al Qaeda and its affiliates. In the past, there has been intense rivalry between them and alliances have usually been tactical and short-lived. We must be ready to work with Islamist groups that have entered the political mainstream in their countries and are competing by legitimate means to enter government. But we should also be clear that their hold on power will be contested by institutions that have existed long before the democratic turn in these countries. Some of these institutions will be important to us in securing and stepping up cooperation on security-related activities like counterterrorism and intelligence.

Related to this is our response to continuing political unrest in various countries of the region. In principle, we continue to support the sovereignty and integrity of these countries, and are averse to use of force by all sides. In practice, though, external intervention will remain a possibility. Our approach therefore has to be a proactive engagement with both the lawfully constituted authority and the democratic forces outside the government, with a view to creating the space for the emergence of a political settlement.

To preclude the possibility of intervention by external powers, we need to go beyond simply reiterating our support for sovereignty and non-intervention. We need to advance strategic arguments in the UN and other forums about the advisability and feasibility of intervention: Is the case for intervention clear-cut? Have all diplomatic options been exhausted? Are there military options that could be sensibly and prudently undertaken? Are the intervening powers prepared for the ensuing transition and the long-haul reconstruction usually required? We also need to be more forthright in contesting the normative justifications advanced by the intervening powers and their rather selective application.

The other key principle that should guide our strategic engagement with West Asia is the avoidance of sharp choices. In particular, we should try and steer clear of the escalating rivalry between Iran and Saudi Arabia. We have major interests in our relationships with both these countries, and need to strike a careful balance in our dealings with each. The acquisition of overt nuclear weapons capability by Iran is undesirable. An additional nuclear weapons state in our strategic neighbourhood will make regional stability more precarious—not least because it may embolden other regional actors to take pre-emptive measures.

The preservation of our economic interests in West Asia will require considerable attention to building up our capabilities in the maritime domain (this is dealt with at greater length in Chapter Three). But we also need to be prepared for a situation where persisting instability in the region results in a steep fall in energy supplies and a sharp rise in prices. We need to carefully monitor our strategic energy reserves and accelerate our efforts to diversify our sources of supply, and expand investment in alternative forms of energy.

East and South-East Asia

India's enhanced engagement with the countries of the Association of Southeast Asian Nations (ASEAN) commenced with the announcement of India's Look East Policy in 1992. From a sectoral dialogue partner, India is now a summit partner of ASEAN. At the India–ASEAN Commemorative Summit held in New Delhi in November 2012, the two sides decided to establish a strategic partnership that will encompass every significant component of our relations with ASEAN—political, security, economic, trade and culture. Our vision should be to revive and reinforce, in a contemporary context, the myriad historical linkages which bound India and the countries of South-East Asia together.

A major asset for our pursuit of India's interests in the region is that virtually all South-East Asian countries welcome a much more enhanced engagement by India, firstly as a significant countervailing security actor, and secondly as a key economic and trade partner, serving as an expanding market and both a source of and a destination for investment. These sentiments are driven by a pervasive, though sometimes muted, anxiety over China's expanding and often assertive presence in the region. This has been accentuated by concerns over the decline in US power and influence despite the recent US 'pivot' to Asia. However, India will have to manage its engagement with South-East Asia in a carefully calibrated manner, since the countries of South-East Asia do not wish to be caught in a crossfire between confronting powers, even as they wish to retain some room for manoeuvre and strategic space vis-à-vis China.

India's policy towards South-East Asia should encompass the following key elements. First, it suits India to have ASEAN maintain its role as the pre-eminent platform through which the emerging economic and security architecture in the region is mediated. Second, India should resist endorsing the Chinese approach of projecting ASEAN+3 (China, Japan and the Republic of Korea) as the 'Core' of the emerging regional order, while consigning the East Asia Summit process to the outer track. Our objective should be to promote a regional order which has space for multiple and parallel forums for pursuing regional integration along variable tracks.

Third, both ASEAN countries and India depend heavily on seaborne trade for their prosperity. This is particularly true of their energy supplies. There are shared concerns over maritime security and India's significant and expanding maritime capabilities will play an important role in shaping a maritime security regime, built upon a set of mutual assurances among the major littoral and user states. Finally, the pursuit of closer economic integration with the region necessitates the rapid development of cross-border connectivity, through roads, railways, airlinks, digital highways and shipping routes. Even while India invests in reconnecting with the countries of South Asia, it must plan these links in the larger context of closer integration with the countries of South-East Asia. India should become a major stakeholder in the ambitious ASEAN Connectivity Initiative.

While emphasizing the primacy of ASEAN as a preferred regional partner, India should, in parallel, pursue a varied diplomacy on the bilateral side. It is obvious that Indonesia, as the largest country in ASEAN, will be a key partner for India in the region. The two countries share a convergent interest in ensuring freedom of navigation and maritime security in the Indian Ocean region. They have common concerns over the challenge which the emergence of China poses for their own respective roles in the region. Indonesia is also an increasingly influential actor in regional and international forums, such as the G-20. This adds to the value of maintaining a strong relationship with the country. The cultural affinity between the peoples of the two countries further enhances the quality of the relationship.

In the context of its Asian diplomacy, India has recognized the importance of Myanmar, which is its gateway to South-East Asia. Myanmar also shares the strategic ocean space of the Bay of Bengal and the Andaman Sea with India. Four of India's key north-eastern states, Arunachal Pradesh, Nagaland, Manipur and Mizoram, lie across the 1400-kilometre-long border with Myanmar. More recently, Myanmar has also emerged as a potential energy partner for India. These factors dictate a policy of high priority to this neighbour to the east, where a rapid, though uncertain, political transformation is under way. The opening up of the country, the diversification of its foreign relations, the flow of investment from multiple sources, all these will serve to diminish the dominant position that China has been able to establish in Myanmar's long period of relative isolation. This can only benefit India.

India must recognize that China will continue to be a significant factor in Myanmar, just as it is in the rest of South-East Asia. However, India has the capacity and resources to establish a strong countervailing presence in the region. In this context, the early implementation of several key cross-border transport corridors is critical to the success of India's Asian diplomacy.

In the case of each ASEAN country, there are particular

aspects of our relationship that can be leveraged. In forging close bilateral relations with Laos, Cambodia and Vietnam, India is a welcome source of human resource development and capacity-building. Vietnam has a much stronger shared concern over China than perhaps some other ASEAN countries and this creates opportunities for a measured increase in India's security profile in Indo-China.

In the case of Singapore, the value of the island country lies in its role as a most convenient and efficient platform for doing business in South-East Asia. More than any other country in the region, it is the most sensitively attuned to the shifts in the balance of power in the region, and it is the country most alert to emerging economic opportunities in the region as well as globally. It can serve as India's weathervane in the region, helping the country to adjust its own strategies in response to the shifts in the regional environment. Singapore will remain a key partner for India in the region.

Japan: In recent years, two key factors have driven India and Japan into a much closer and expanded relationship: the concern over China and the economic opportunity that India offers to a depressed Japanese economy. The steady increase in the security and defence relationship between the two countries is a new factor in regional security and is welcome since it gives India greater strategic space in the region. The maritime dimension of the security relationship will be the most important, dependent as the two countries are on the safety of their extended sea lines of communication (SLOC). This growing security relationship must be managed and constantly calibrated so as to act as a constraint on China without provoking hostile countermeasures. This will require finely nuanced policies from both countries.

Japan has great value for India as a source of capital and high technology. Unlike in the past, Japanese government and business are seriously looking at India as a major investment destination and economic partner. However, there remain concerns over India's uncertain investment climate, red-tapism and poor infrastructure. Unless these constraints are swiftly addressed, a moment of significant opportunity and a major boost to India's growth story may be lost.

Korean Peninsula: In the early 1990s, South Korea overtook Japan in recognizing and exploiting the opportunities created by India's economic reform and liberalization process. Today, South Korean companies have a major presence in India and their profile continues to expand. Japanese companies are still trying to catch up. South Korea has also emerged as an important source of sophisticated technology, including in defence hardware. The more recent tensions in China–South Korea relations have also created political opportunities for India, driving a closer security relationship between the two countries.

North Korea has been a source of clandestine nuclear and missile proliferation to Pakistan, with China widely suspected of playing a supportive role. This makes developments on the Korean Peninsula a matter of considerable interest to India. It is also true that any major political disruption on the peninsula, such as the collapse of the North Korean regime, may set into motion major geopolitical changes. A reunified Korea under a democratic and prosperous South Korea would be the best eventual outcome from an Indian perspective. This may be the least preferred outcome for China and perhaps even Japan. A Chinese intervention in North Korea in response to its political collapse may set into motion a much wider confrontation and conflict in the region. This would adversely affect Indian interests as well. Given these possible scenarios, a closer engagement by India on the Korean issue may be worthwhile.

Taiwan: India has acknowledged that Taiwan is a part of China. Nevertheless, it has, like several other countries, maintained trade and non-official relations with Taiwan. Despite its political isolation, Taiwan has emerged as a regional economic powerhouse and the source of sophisticated technologies particularly in the information and communications technology sector. India has been slow in taking advantage of the opportunities that Taiwan offers, particularly in its hesitancy in allowing some political- and official-level relations, without inviting Chinese hostility. Yet, given that China itself is permitting ministerial- level exchanges with Taiwan, there is no reason why India should maintain its own relations with Taiwan at a level lower than what China itself pursues.

Taiwan also has value for India as an excellent source of information on China and for pursuit of China-related research and studies. As China's regional and global profile increases, the value of offshore China-watching centres like Taiwan, Singapore and Hong Kong has greatly increased, since China remains relatively opaque despite its recent openness.

Central Asia

The third pillar of India's Asian strategy is Central Asia. Unlike West and East Asia, with which India has contiguous land and/or sea access, Central Asia is separated from India by the territory of Pakistan and its illegally occupied territory of Jammu and Kashmir.

Pakistan does not allow access to Afghanistan and beyond to Central Asia through this territory, compelling India to seek a much more circuitous and difficult access through Iran. Nevertheless, Central Asia, in particular Afghanistan, Kazakhstan, Uzbekistan, Tajikistan and other countries in the region, are important to India for reasons of historical and cultural affinity, as potential sources of energy supplies, in particular natural gas, and as markets for Indian goods and services.

Central Asia is also a strategic theatre where Chinese influence is steadily expanding. It is likely to challenge the currently dominant position of Russia in what the latter regards as its 'near abroad'. For this reason too it is a region of considerable significance for an emerging power like India. The challenge for India will lie in eventually obtaining access to Afghanistan and the Central Asian heartland through Pakistan, even while continuing to improve and upgrade the current transportation link via Iran. Pakistan will need to be persuaded that the negative leverage it exercises against India through denial of transit is outweighed by the positive benefits it could derive through serving as a bridge between India and Central Asia.

CHAPTER 2

India and the International Order

International Economic Engagement

India's integration into the global economy is vital to its continued prosperity. The international context represents a huge opportunity for India. India must recognize both that the foundations of its power will, in a large part, depend upon the economic footprint it will have on the world and that it has more to gain from globalizing its economy than it has to fear. In short, globalization presents India with more opportunities than risks. But at the same time, India has to recognize that those countries gain most from globalization that have put their own house in order.

India's global economic engagement has to pursue two tracks simultaneously. On the one hand, India has to take advantage of its human capital and become a hub for low-cost manufacturing and services. Our ability to do so will depend upon our domestic laws and regulations, and our ability to invest effectively in infrastructure and human capital. But there is every reason to believe that with modest reforms and political stability, India can be a very attractive destination for investors in its manufacturing capacity.

But India also has the potential to become a hub for high-end technology and value-added services. The twenty-first century will belong to economies that are at the cutting edge of technological innovation. It is difficult to imagine a technologically innovative economy that is not also an open economy. Competing in the international economy can be a spur to innovation, it can allow easy assimilation of technology and it has the potential of converting India into a research and development hub.

Domestically there will be some losers in the process of globalization. We should by no means overlook this fact. But India has the potential of globalizing in ways that minimize its costs. For one thing, India has to ensure that it does not globalize in a way that artificially represses domestic consumption. Second, some of the gains from growth have to be leveraged by the state to build a social safety net that can mitigate social risk. There need not be any contradiction between globalization and building a social safety net. At India's stage of development the two are reciprocally connected. Growth will allow safety nets to be built. And social safety nets will in turn ensure that we are in a position to take advantage of the global economy, and socially better able to weather some of its risks and uncertainties.

While the opportunities for India are immense, we should be clear-eyed about the potential complexities we have to navigate. The global economy is entering unchartered waters. A series of crises in Europe and America, emerging challenges for the Chinese economy, the rise of new competitors in Africa and other parts of Asia, all portend an uncertain decade of adjustment and readjustment. The global economy will see major realignments at different levels. Patterns of trade and manufacturing will continue to shift. The future of the dollar as a reserve currency is open for question. The architecture of global economic governance will be severely contested.

It follows that many of the intellectual premises that have shaped globalization over the last couple of decades will be questioned. Domestic political pressure in advanced economies may lead to more trade and immigration restrictions. The legitimacy of capital mobility will be seriously contested. Different national interests may make it difficult to create a global economic architecture based on consensus. In short, countries may not continue to view globalization as a non-zero sum game.

Internally too, each of the major economies is in a period of adjustment. Europe and Japan face, among other things, the challenge of an ageing population. Advanced economies will struggle to redefine and sustain their social protections. Governments may resort to industrial policy as a conscious policy tool. These patterns and trends are uncertain. But paying closer attention to the domestic policy choices of other countries, and determining how we can capitalize on them by our own policy choices, may afford India huge economic opportunities which could override the challenges posed by uncertainties in the developed economies.

India's primary strategic interest therefore is to ensure an open economic order. While India has often been accused of being protectionist in the past, current events have left India on the better side of liberalization arguments. Thus, India might end up becoming one of the more prominent supporters of continued economic liberalization (primarily trade in goods and services, and possibly finance as well). India needs to start taking a more active role in bilateral and multilateral forums to ensure that the world economic order remains open. One step in this direction that may be feasible is the establishment of multiple bilateral FTAs, especially with the countries that currently contribute the greatest amount to global growth (Brazil,

China, South Africa, Turkey, Indonesia and Nigeria).

To a certain extent, there is a trade-off between pursuing openness through multilateral institutions and pursuing them through bilateral ones. In many ways bilateral agreements are a 'second' best. But they are easier to pursue than complex multilateral agreements. Yet India will need to ensure that its preference for bilateral agreements is not simply because it prefers the easy way out. Multilateral agreements remain an important goal, and will require greater domestic consensus-building.

One strategic reason to maintain a greater emphasis on multilateral forums centres on China. It is very important that China remains tethered to a fair multilateral system, and a rule-bound international order. In that context, India's own commitments to multilateralism can help to promote a rule-bound system. India's opting out, or placing less importance on successful multilateral negotiations (even if the short-term costs seem high), may have effects on the whole system. So on a range of issues—currency, trade, finance—India needs to consider its options in the light of these changing realities and imperatives.

Besides trade openness, India will have to push for greater mobility of people. It should possibly take a lead in innovative totalization agreements and tax treaties that allow movement of labour and human capital. India has a possible advantage in services. India also needs to resist non-trade-related protectionism. A likely backdoor form of protectionism on the part of the developed economies is going to be a push for environmental standards and labour-related regulations. While India should commit to and enforce such environmental regimes and labour standards as are best for its population, it will have to build coalitions against arbitrary restrictions that amount to trade protection in disguise.

India should also formulate policy in relation to cutting-edge areas like natural resource export protectionism. The recent controversy over rare earth materials is just a reminder that natural resource protectionism may become a tool in international negotiations. Further, India needs to take a more proactive role in international regimes to control illicit finance. Illicit flows of funds and money laundering have economic and security consequences. It is in India's interest to ensure that there is global coordination on bank transparency, money laundering and tax havens.

On questions of the mobility of goods, services, capital and labour, at present India's restrictions greatly exceed those seen in the median G-20 nations. Hence, the domestic liberalization process continues to be important and must be pursued, since India gains from unilateral liberalization, and also because India will not be taken seriously in the global debate on an open global order until it achieves above-median openness by the standards of G-20 nations. Notions of reciprocity should not be allowed to interfere with the more purely domestic agenda of removal of trade barriers. At the same time, India's effective participation in global negotiations on an open world order will require bargaining chips. India will have to make difficult choices about what it is willing to put on the negotiating agenda.

Meeting this set of strategic imperatives rests on domestic political skills and judgements. Ideally all international norms of openness rest on reciprocity. India needs to preserve openness globally—and so it should be prepared to extend that opennesss to the domestic economy. Here, the challenge in our international negotiations has not often been lack of domestic consensus. It has rather been the inordinate veto power given to small lobbies or special interests. Their legitimate concerns need to be taken into account. But these should not be used as a pretext for stalling internal reforms that are vital.

India needs international investment for its own domestic growth. Indeed, India's investment needs in vital sectors like infrastructure and defence are vast.

Given the instant mobility of global capital, increasingly in search of beneficial investment locations, it is in our strategic interest to attract as much foreign direct investment (FDI) as possible. Such FDI not only serves our domestic needs, but also gives us strategic leverage with other countries.

It is important that India's FDI policy should be geared to enhancing the domestic knowledge base as well. In areas like defence, leveraging FDI for technology and knowledge access has been tried, but so far with very modest results. Corporate entities (both public and private sector) that enter into large-scale contracts with foreign entities must be able to use the scale of their investments to ensure that India benefits from technology or skills transfer (especially from countries hit by the recent financial crisis). This is particularly true of defence offsets, which have historically focused on low value-added activities. Access to technology and intellectual property issues will also arise in this process.

In the near future, managing India's current account deficit is going to be a challenge, at two levels. First, no power can grow only by exporting, in the main, services or natural resources. India's exports need to be more balanced. Second, our own domestic infrastructure requirements are likely to require significant imports.

Indeed, in many of the vital areas of manufacturing, from capital equipment to semi-conductors, India does not have adequate manufacturing capacity. The fact that we need to import can be a source of bargaining. But it is also a source of vulnerability and constrains our options.

We need continuous analysis and engagement with the future of the global monetary system. In particular, the possible decline of the US dollar and the somewhat inevitable relative rise of the Chinese yuan have major implications for how India orients its investment and reserve strategies. What should we be doing with our capital controls and limited convertibility in the long run? India is well positioned in this debate, given that the rupee has become a floating exchange rate from early 2009 onward, and that exchange restrictions have been greatly relaxed over the past two decades. This is a contrast to China and shows India as a responsible participant in the global economy. In addition, this has given India an edge in developing institutional capabilities in both monetary policy and finance. These propitious initial conditions imply that India may have an even better starting point (when compared to China) for policies that would be conducive to the emergence of the rupee as an international currency. Should India be ambitious and go down this route? Or should it let the terms of financial engagement be exogenously set? To what extent are certain necessary domestic reforms dependent on taking a strategic view of the global monetary order?

India's own financial sector is of paramount strategic importance. India has been prudent in charting its own path in this sector. Unlike most countries who are net importers of financial services, India is already a significant exporter of financial services and has a potential international financial centre in Mumbai. But we face a basic question: In view of the likely scenarios in the global financial world, what reforms will best position us to take advantage of emerging opportunities? Globally, the financial sector's recent performance has attracted justified scepticism. As we seek to position ourselves as a financial hub, we shall need to balance prudence with bold innovation, so as to mitigate risks. The range of possible policy choices remains wide. But we do need a national consensus on at least this basic proposition: our choices in finance should not be made purely based on short-term crisis management considerations. They must be based on an understanding of the strategic value of a developed, globally oriented financial sector.

The fact that pressures on imports are likely to remain may also make it tempting to manage current account deficits by encouraging flows of 'hot money'. But as far as possible, India should encourage FDI, and not solve structural problems by short-term measures that may carry large costs later. Managing the current account will also require us to be inventive in encouraging new instruments like bilateral currency swaps.

We will need to devise a clear view of what kind of role we wish to play in the international economic order. Very important decisions that we are taking—capital account convertibility, the structure of banking reform, the creation of bond markets, exchange rate policies—are driven by immediate domestic concerns. While this may to some extent be inevitable, it is imperative that we keep firmly in mind the strategic consequences of such choices: Are we a net debtor or a net creditor? Do we have pretensions of having our currency among a basket of reserve currencies? Many policy options will depend on how we answer these questions.

Indian capital is itself rapidly going global. The reasons driving this are complex, but there are clear strategic consequences here too. What, for instance, will be the Indian state's relationship to Indian private capital abroad? India's diplomacy will have to be increasingly geared to serve its commercial as well as its other interests.

Our internal fiscal system needs to evolve considerably if it is to support India's international aspirations. The goods and services tax (GST), along with full integration of imports and exports (where imports are charged the domestic GST and exports are zero-rated, thus refunding the entire burden of domestic indirect taxation), will make a major difference to trade in goods and services. The shift to residence-based taxation will bring India on a par with the countries of the Organisation for Economic Co-operation and Development (OECD) and all sophisticated emerging markets on the treatment of capital flows, as opposed to the present Mauritius treaty. Special efforts need to be undertaken on appropriate tax treatment of Indians working abroad for part of the year, and on non-residents working in India for part of the year.

Agriculture has been a vexed issue for India. The domestic political implications of agriculture sector liberalization are uncertain. The external dimension of agriculture will be shaped by two contexts. Food security is going to be on the agenda of several major economies, as fears of food price inflation spread. It is in India's interest that the global regime on food trade be fair and open. Global cooperation on food security will be of fundamental importance. Second, the gradual elimination of agriculture subsidies in the United States and Europe may bring agriculture liberalization back on the agenda. Agriculture liberalization is a difficult area for us. It has complex social and economic consequences. But India needs to carefully weigh its options, and to have a clear long-term strategy in this area—one that is not merely susceptible to short-term political pressures. Here too, we need to evolve greater agreement on long-term management of the agriculture sector, leading to a national consensus on its strategic importance, particularly in an era of uncertainty in global food commodities markets.

Our international economic integration will require partners in the immediate neighbourhood. This will need a concerted push towards increasing mobility of goods, services, capital and labour needs vis-à-vis the countries of South Asia, East Africa, West Asia and South-East Asia: all of which are well positioned to dramatically expand their economic engagement with India. Within modest time horizons, it should be possible to enlarge measures of integration with these countries by ten times, on all four dimensions (goods, services, capital and labour).

All these areas will require institutional collaboration and redesign. Our government, political and business elites still tend to think of the international economy in terms of discrete issue areas of concern to each of them. That fragmented picture must be abandoned, in favour of one that views our international economic engagements as a unified and coherent project—embodying shared interests and with clear linkages back into the domestic economy and electoral considerations. Can we leverage bargains from one sector to the other? Do we possess the institutional mechanisms to do so? There already exist many government institutions that should ideally address these questions (within the Ministry of External Affairs, Ministry of Finance, Ministry of Commerce, Reserve Bank of India, etc.). However, lateral communication between these institutions is too often blocked and insufficient. Appropriate intergovernmental communication must be enhanced, while avoiding bureaucratic creep: effective coordinating mechanisms between various actors would be a first step.

Second, there is a major shortage of systemic, continuous data collection activities which should provide the empirical basis for strategic decisions. Such activities need to be started immediately—perhaps with the help of India's burgeoning knowledge-processing industry. In this vein, given rapid developments in information collection and processing technologies, there will need to be regular reassessment of what activities are best allocated to the public and private sectors respectively. Bureaucratically entrenched data and analysis systems are no longer adequate to our current and coming strategic requirements concerning the economy.

Third, the form of interaction between the public and private sector needs fundamental change. Generally speaking, the government and Indian businesses seem to have a fairly instrumental relationship, with each side conversing with the other only in times of crisis or need. What is needed is a sustained, collaborative dialogue, where trust can be built and both sides can develop realistic notions of what they can and cannot expect from the other. Such a relationship would greatly augment the strategic coordination possible between government and business, both internationally and domestically. Greater continuous communication on economic issues between government and the business community should in turn be transparent to the media, so that public opinion can be carried along in creating a national consensus on our strategic economic interests.

India must have a coherent vision of the global economy and its position within it, combined with a concrete set of actions for its interactions in various international institutions which are part of the global economic order. This includes not only the International Monetary Fund (IMF) and World Bank, but also international standards organizations like the Basel agreements, accounting standards, G-20, etc. While it may not be necessary to take an aggressive stance in every organization or institution, the scenario building and consideration of strategic options seem to be severely lacking (as is evidenced, for instance, by India's role in such processes as appointments of IMF chiefs). In each of these international engagements, India needs to boost the intellectual capacity within the country which would identify India's interests on an array of issues and help the government strategize mechanisms through which India's interests can be pursued.

Partnerships in a Global Context

India's engagement in the construction of an international order will be through a variety of instruments: participation in regional and global institutions and possible participation with groups of countries. The structures of competition in the global system will present India with a range of partnership choices. For a start, India will be sought after in great power competition. This presents a great historical opportunity for India. Traditionally India has been uneasy about formal alliances. But when national interest has required it, we have chosen closer relationships with particular powers. Yet this has been done while maintaining the core objectives of nonalignment: maintaining strategic autonomy; protecting core national interests; and, as far as possible, maintaining India's position as an object of great power agreement. These broad objectives remain valid. But they will have to be interpreted and pursued in a new context.

At no time since the emergence of a recognizable 'world system' has power been so diffused at the global level. India's own position will need to be able to straddle many worlds, to connect across the various nodes of a more diffused global power system. In terms of constitutional vision, India is the most 'Western' and liberal among the non-Western powers. But we are rooted in Asia. As a poor and developing country, we also have an enormous global footprint. We have the potential to become a technological powerhouse, yet remain an informal economy. We are committed to democratic practices and are convinced that robust democracies are a surer guarantee of security in our neighbourhood and beyond. Yet we do not 'promote' democracy or see it as an ideological concept that serves as a polarizing axis in world politics. It follows that there are few 'natural' groupings—whether defined by political vision, economic profile and interests, or geopolitical security challenges—into which India can seamlessly fit. This diverse identity and the multiple interests that it underpins are actually our greatest strategic assets at the global level. For it means that India can be a unique bridge between different worlds. Indeed, India's bridging potential is one we must leverage and turn to our active benefit.

It is often said that India is well placed to improve its relations with all powers simultaneously, and this has also been our experience in the past decade. But such an approach also poses real challenges and demands skilful diplomacy. For example, in the foreseeable future India will need to calibrate its value to the United States as a countervailing power vis-à-vis China, with the need to avoid provoking China into open and damaging confrontation.

The partnership game, if played delicately, can yield real benefits. The prospect that India is a potential partner can give it leverage, both with the country courting it and with potential rivals. India must leverage to the full extent possible this dual diplomatic potential. Overall though, it is undoubtedly in India's best interests to have a deep and wide engagement with as many powers as are willing to engage with it. This engagement is important for developing our own technology and military capabilities, as well as for spreading economic risks and for benefiting from flows of ideas and innovation distinctive to particular cultural traditions and contexts.

Such broad international engagement is also important

as a hedge against possible contingency. In the past, it has often been the force of events that has pushed India into closer relationships with other powers. Given that the future of Sino-US relations is uncertain, and that the likely evolution of China's own foreign policy remains unclear, India must be prepared for a contingency where, for instance, threatening behaviour by one of the major powers could encourage or even force it to be closer to another. This is still a low-probability event, but cannot be ruled out entirely. India should engage with a variety of powers. But it has to recognize that its core security challenges are ones that it has to meet alone.

United States

The United States of America remains the single most powerful country in the world. Its economic and military capabilities and its global reach remain unmatched. Its long-term prospects are better than that of most other advanced, industrialized economies, despite the current financial and economic crisis impacting the developed world. The United States has a favourable demography; it remains the knowledge capital of the world; its technological capabilities and culture of innovation continue to create value; and its entrepreneurial class is one of the world's most dynamic. For India, a closer partnership with the United States is both indispensable and desirable, in its journey towards achieving its own ambitious economic and social objectives.

India–US partnership is further strengthened by shared democratic values, intangible but important in sustaining India's image in the United States as a friendly, benign and non-threatening power. A large and successful Indo-American community has served as a valuable bridge linking the two peoples together. There is a negative legacy of the past which continues to linger in the Indian consciousness. For most of the Cold War years, the United States bent its overwhelming power to frustrate Indian ambitions, ring it with ever-tightening technology denial regimes and remained unmindful of the collateral damage it inflicted on India due to its alliance with Pakistan and, later, with its quasi-alliance with China. However, the international environment which motivated negative US policies towards India has been transformed since the end of the Cold War and continues to witness rapid change. India should be mindful of history; its caution regarding the United States may be well founded. However, the legacy of history should not become a millstone round our necks, feeding into prejudice. This will prevent India from deriving advantage from the changed international environment and leveraging a positive, forward-looking and friendly partnership with the United States in advancing our own strategic objectives.

If, in the past, a hostile United States could constrain India's room for manoeuvre, today, in the unfolding international landscape, a strong India–US partnership, properly handled, can expand India's strategic space. This has been evident in the strategic gain that India has achieved through the Indo-US Civil Nuclear Agreement. The current deterioration of US–Pakistan relations, with the prospect of US withdrawal from Afghanistan, further reinforces the convergence in India–US relations.

While US pre-eminence is likely to remain undiminished for the foreseeable future, its relative power and influence have and will continue to decline due to the rise of several other powers. At the upper tier, China and India will continue to expand as will Brazil. Russia and Japan may witness further relative decline in the global pecking order, while Europe will undergo relative decline more slowly. Middle-rung powers like South Korea, Indonesia, Turkey, Egypt, Iran and South Africa will gain in power and influence. Over the horizon, Africa and Latin America seem likely to emerge as the economic powerhouses of the future.

This rise of the Rest has inevitably led to the diffusion of political and economic power, though in a somewhat asymmetric manner. The US alliance system is weakening. Its closest allies in Europe and Japan are no longer the strong and predictable pillars of US global strategy as they were in the past. The search for a viable strategy has led the United States to build or renew partnerships with countries like India, Indonesia, Brazil and South Africa. However, these relationships are being pursued in a world very different from the Cold War era—when the Soviet 'threat' led some of these countries to seek US support and assurance of security. In contrast, the world's rising powers see greater opportunity in playing the polycentric game. Instead of fixed and stable alliances there are ad hoc region- or issue-based coalitions. The United States, which has been used to dealing with allies or with adversaries, has been finding it difficult to adjust to more nuanced relationships with the rising powers. India–US relations display some of these contradictions.

China is America's principal competitor, more in economic terms and less, for the time being, in military terms. In this context, India holds special attraction for the United States because, after China, it is the biggest among rising powers and has a complex, and often adversarial, relationship with China. Nevertheless, there are two competing trends in the evolving US posture towards China. One seeks to reconcile the United States to the inevitability of Chinese ascendancy in the Asian theatre, and position it as an offshore balancer. This harks back to the role, in the nineteenth century, of the United Kingdom vis-à-vis the European continent. The other trend of thinking seeks to contain China as a threat to US dominance, with the Asia-Pacific theatre being regarded as critical to maintaining US pre-eminence globally. US policy appears to oscillate between these two ends of the spectrum, currently being closer to the latter end of the spectrum. For India, Sino-US collusion is as much of a threat as is the prospect of their open confrontation. While the United States could, in certain circumstances, emerge as a likely ally, for the present, Indian interests may be better served by a strong and broad-based partnership with the United States while managing the dynamic mix of competition and convergence in India–China relations.

Europe

India has been an enthusiastic supporter of the idea of united Europe, seeing in European integration a trend towards the multipolarity that India has instinctively favoured over the past several decades. Europe is an undervalued and neglected target of Indian engagement. Despite its current economic weakness and diminished security consensus, Europe is, and will remain, a major political actor and economic and technological powerhouse. The European Union is, like India, a multi-ethnic, multicultural and multilingual plural democracy. Both sides have a mutual stake in each other's success so as to firmly anchor democratic and liberal values in a world increasingly threatened by extremist and exclusivist tendencies. There is a much higher level of comfort in pursuing closer engagement and collaboration with Europe even in sensitive areas such as defence. Europe is and will remain a major source of high-end technologies and a partner for capacity-building and skill development in India. Therefore, policy towards Europe must remain an indispensable part of any long-term Indian strategy.

While upgrading its relationship with the European Union, India has maintained close bilateral links with each of the major actors in the region, in particular, the United Kingdom, France and Germany. The focus on these major European powers has led to the neglect of the smaller countries in Europe, in particular the new members of the erstwhile socialist bloc of East European nations. These countries retain their goodwill and positive sentiments for India from the days of our privileged relations with the socialist bloc. We have not been able to leverage this asset to our advantage. Our policy towards Europe could benefit from a renewed focus on these countries, which have much to offer to India in terms of trade, investment as well as technology. For example, the Czech Republic and Slovakia could be tapped as suppliers of several defence-related technologies without the conditionalities that other suppliers may impose.

The current economic turmoil in Europe is a matter of grave concern to India. The weakening of integrated Europe, its possible fragmentation and its economic decline will have far-reaching geopolitical consequences. As a force for stability and as a bastion of democratic and liberal values, the European Union is of great value to India. Its weakening will have adverse consequences for India as well. Europe is preoccupied with dealing with its ongoing crisis and has lately become more inward-looking. India should support the strengthening of the European Union both as an economic and as a political entity as the preferred means for dealing with the crisis. The survival of the euro as a strong alternative reserve currency to the US dollar is also in India's interest.

The balance of power within the European Union is changing. Germany is emerging unmistakably as the most powerful and influential member of the union. The United Kingdom is likely to see its own role progressively diluted, whether it accepts the discipline of a stronger European Union or if it decides to loosen its links with continental Europe. It is clear that Germany must enjoy greater priority and attention in our European policy, even while we continue to maintain our traditionally strong links with the United Kingdom and France.

Russia

It would be fair to say that India and the then Soviet Union enjoyed a strategic partnership between 1960 and 1990, despite being very different political systems. The strategic glue was the shared perception of threat from China, but there were other motivations driving the relationship as well. The Soviet Union valued the Non-Aligned Movement and India's leading role in the movement as preventing the strategic encirclement of the Soviet Union through a ring of US-led alliance systems. For India, the Soviet Union's support on the Kashmir issue, the extension of Soviet assistance to India's economic development and, significantly, its willingness to share defence hardware and technology with India at a time when the West had virtually turned off the taps were of critical importance.

With the end of the Cold War and the emergence of Russia as a more diminished power, there has been a significant change in the nature of India–Russia relations. Trade has become insignificant, the China factor is no longer a driving force in the relations, but the defence hardware relationship remains robust, though India is beginning to diversify its sources of supply. The political relationship continues to be nurtured by regular summits between the leaders; and Russia, it is hoped, will also become a significant energy partner for India. The Russian connection is useful in terms of India's efforts to build broad coalitions of emerging powers to pursue convergent objectives. Thus, India should embrace the opportunity to work together with Russia in BRICS, in the India–China–Russia trilateral, in the Shanghai Cooperation Organization and in the G-20. However, there is little prospect of a return to the strategic partnership that endured for three decades during the Cold War. The world that gave rise to that partnership no longer exists.

Africa

Africa is the continent of the future. No long-term strategy formulated by any major power can neglect the opportunities offered by a vast, resource-rich continent, which has lately been undergoing a significant and sustained political and economic transformation. In the midst of deepening economic gloom across the globe, Africa as a whole has been able to sustain an overall GDP growth rate of over 6 per cent per annum. As the process of national consolidation and infrastructure development continues apace, African countries may well emerge as 'emerging economies' of tomorrow.

China has made deep inroads into Africa but its focus has been on resource exploitation and raw material extraction. India's engagement has been more broad-based and has covered a wide spectrum of trade, investment, capacity development and infrastructure assistance. However, while this has generated widespread goodwill for India, political exchanges have not kept pace with the level and potential of economic engagement. This has created a perception of India's lack of interest and even neglect of African countries compared to its focus on other regions of the world. This needs to be remedied.

Currently, there is inordinate focus on relations with South Africa, while neglecting other major actors such as Nigeria and Ghana, Kenya, Uganda and Tanzania. The engagement with French-speaking Africa is particularly weak, as it is also with lusophone Africa—whose countries possess resources of significant interest to India. It is necessary therefore to pursue a more diversified and well-balanced policy towards Africa, recognizing the differential potential that each country represents.

Latin America

The Latin American continent currently lies outside the strategic footprint of India, but it is gaining in importance as a source of key resources, in particular energy supplies. It is also an expanding market for Indian goods and services. The information technology (IT) industry has made notable inroads into the continent.

Brazil has emerged as India's most privileged partner in Latin America. Bilateral trade and investment have been increasing steadily. They are pursuing an energy partnership, with India seeking a stake in offshore hydrocarbon exploration in Brazilian waters. Defence and nuclear energy are other areas where the potential for bilateral cooperation is significant. It is a relationship that has a dimension beyond a bilateral level. The two countries have drawn closer together as emerging economies with similar aspirations, including their claim to permanent membership of the UN Security Council. Along with South Africa, they have consolidated the IBSA group of democratic nations. They work together in multilateral forums like the WTO, the UN Framework Convention on Climate Change (UNFCCC) and the G-20.

India has pursued closer relations with other major countries in Latin America, including Mexico, Argentina and Chile. In these cases too the bilateral relationship is reinforced by their cooperation in multilateral forums.

The outlook for the future is a steady growth in India's engagement with Latin America, with relations with Brazil remaining its centerpiece.

International Institutions

Engagement with international institutions has been integral to India's foreign and strategic policy. But India will now have to engage with, and respond to, these institutions in new contexts that are themselves shifting.

The first element of this new context is the sheer number of institutions. There has been an exponential growth in new institutions, summit processes and interstate groupings. Stretching across the world today is a thicket of regional, global and functional institutions. Servicing the commitments entailed by participation in these international institutions requires an outlay of resources and the ability to draw on appropriate expertise. In fact, making full strategic use of the opportunities afforded by these institutions depends to a great extent on capacity. And India's capacities are currently lagging well behind its commitments.

What is, of course, driving the proliferation of new institutions is the fact that our inherited global bodies like the UN or the Bretton Woods institutions, all creations of the post–Second World War political settlements, are constricted by the circumstances of their origins. They are the creatures of an era still dominated by the West, and quite inappropriate for a world that has seen the end of the European empires and the rise of Asia's economic dynamism. These institutions require fundamental reform to reflect the new distribution of power in the world. India must actively pursue a more influential role in these institutions—a position commensurate not just with its growing power but also with its expanding range of global interests. India's claim to active participation in these institutions will importantly rest on the fact that its own interests are impinged upon by the decisions of these institutions and therefore it must have a full voice in decision-making. We can expect the reform process to be gradual, but we should continue to push it along.

The third major change in context is that different institutions are actively competing for legitimacy. And in turn there is competition among nations for entry into several of these new institutions and groupings. Faced with the proliferation of international clubs, India will have to take some important decisions as to which institutions to lend its weight and commitment: whether at the regional, trans-regional or global level.

It is right that as India's stature rises, it should seek to reshape the global order by influencing and reshaping international institutions. But we will also face a basic dilemma—which all rising and great powers have faced. Should such powers lend their weight to global institutions, even if it means occasionally adverse consequences for themselves? Or should they practise a politics of great power exceptionalism, where multilateral institutions matter only in so far as they are a medium of projecting national power? In practice the choices are not so stark. But there are occasional trade-offs between a single-minded pursuit of national interest and investment in the legitimacy of global institutions. We will have to protect our core national interests. But the world will be looking to see how much we choose to invest in strengthening the legitimacy and authority of international institutions. Handling this altered context will require India to make some wise choices, about where to apportion political capital.

India will continue deep engagement with the UN. A permanent seat on the UN Security Council is a desirable objective. India should recognize that time is on its side in this matter. As the structure of global power shifts, India's case inevitably becomes stronger. But India will also, in the interim, have to demonstrate a leadership capacity to propose solutions to and artfully handle some of the difficult challenges facing the world.

India's engagement with the UN will continue to be at several levels, and will also pose new questions for our policies. There is, for instance, often a trade-off between investment in bilateral engagements and the commitment of resources to multilateral institutions. On the one hand, bilateral aid is usually more flexible, and the donor is also more clearly identifiable and visible to the recipient. On the other hand, multilateral institutions like the UN are often less flexible, and donor identity is not highlighted, but participation in their programme budgets can enable India to shape the global agenda. While there are real trade-offs, particularly in terms of beneficial use of resources, India's best option is to engage at different levels, and to use different levers.

International engagement can have real impact on domestic capabilities. India's human resources receive exposure to best international practices, and these can feed back into domestic governance structures and cultures. The Comptroller and Auditor General's participation in

UN audit processes, has, for example, enhanced its own capacities.

India will also need to recognize more fully that much of today's global norm-setting is not done by formal institutions, but rather by informal networks of professionals: non-governmental organizations (NGOs), lawyers, bankers, heads of industry. These informal networks are beginning to have a profound impact on the functioning of formal institutions. We will, at the level of the Indian state, need to find ways of interacting with these informal networks, playing a role in their debates and working to influence outcomes.

India is operating in a context where rapidly growing economies like China have become substantial bilateral donors. Such new donor states have also got the ability to invest immense resources in the creation of new institutions. The entrance of new donor states, and donor competition between them and the old donor states, is a feature of the new global economic landscape. While India is now bulking up and systematizing its aid programme, more attention and resources will need to be devoted to this. This aid could potentially open strategic opportunities and spaces.

For India, G-20 will remain an important new institution. It is true that the future of G-20 is very much in the balance. After playing a powerful role in response to the financial crisis, it has been 'missing in action'. It is an open question whether this is because of a particular conjuncture in world and domestic political cycles, where almost all leaders are burdened with domestic problems. At one level, this has led to a less effective G-20. But at another level, this could be an opportunity for India to show some leadership. And G-20 may be the right forum to do it—even if it proves to be a transitional one, it provides a platform for India to show some of its capacities to shape and define agendas.

G-20 (or something like it) may remain important, because it is the only forum where we have an equal voice. The grouping is, strictly speaking, not representative. But it has countries of sufficient weight to be able to carry the rest of the world: it enjoys a degree of legitimacy. What it lacks is sufficient consensus among the G-20 members, in part a result of its conjunction of developed and emerging economies, with their different interests. India does not see the G-20 as a substitute for other formal established institutions. Rather, it offers us a strategic platform and an opportunity to take the lead and to demonstrate how a new leadership association of this type can serve as a template for steering committees in other multilateral institutions—such as the UN or the IMF.

Given the complex nature of India's interests, we will have to ensure that India has access to, or membership in, all the relevant forums that affect its interests. It also follows that we shall need to press for open and inclusive governance architectures and decision-making structures with these institutions.

India's objective will be to play an active role in international institutions. But as it adopts this role, it necessarily follows that it will be increasingly asked to spell out its position on international norms. For long, India largely resisted norms and regimes that it saw as the vehicles of great power dominance. But as India grows more prominent, it will have to define a more positive vision of international norms and rules—and decide what norms to throw its weight behind.

India has also benefited from its engagement with new institutions and groupings like IBSA and BRICS. These ought to be made more robust, while simultaneously newer avenues of strategic engagement should be added: such as the Indian Ocean Region (going beyond the Indian Ocean Naval Symposium), Turkey, Indonesia, Iran, the Gulf Cooperation Council (GCC), 'Dialogue of Civilisations', among others. Not all of these can be expected to be equally effective; but our active engagement with each of them should be seen as part of a strategy of broadening our options and arenas in which we can exercise influence for different purposes.

International institutions that have an Africa focus should be of particular interest for India in both economic and political terms. India cannot match China in terms of investible resources and aid for Africa but its own equities are not inconsiderable: human resources, health and medicine, soft power, institution building, low-cost technology-driven solutions. Powers like the US may seek to piggyback on Indian equities in emerging areas like Africa. Working within international organizations concerned with Africa has upsides and downsides, both of which need careful evaluation. Above all, India should recognize that Africa is itself looking to leverage its relation with other major powers, and this gives India opportunities to enlarge its strategic space.

International Law and Norms

India must recognize and take advantage of its own extraordinary history in the evolution of international law and norms. It was an active participant in the creation of modern human rights norms. It has stood for a world order that was more equitable, just and non-discriminatory. It has been a major advocate of more rational security structures.

Norms do matter in international society. Nation states will, for the foreseeable future, remain the principal units of international society. But nation states—even those with the ability to enforce their will—operate within a context of international public opinion and norms. For all the emphasis on national power, the fact remains that, over the long duration of history, norms have come to be institutionalized in the international system, and have come to regulate wide areas of interstate behaviour.

Norms in the international system often mask the exercise of raw power. They are also hostage to the fact that enforcement of these norms is selective. It is often a pretext for the application of power. And even when the intentions are benign, judgements about what precise action is required in order to enforce a norm remain disputable. Any discourse on norms not allied with prudence can be self-defeating.

But equally there is no denying that the evolution of norms has largely been governed by a progressive agreement over certain moral imperatives: from the prohibition of slavery, the institutionalization of human rights, to the end of apartheid. It is therefore essential when thinking about international norms to have a clear diagnosis of the demand for these norms.

This is of particular importance for us, since the world

will be increasingly looking to India to shape global norms. Rather than being a passive observer, it is in India's interests to proactively shape the evolution of these norms and the contexts of their application. This will require considerable investment in diplomatic and intellectual capacity. For example, India's ability to engage with and shape international law is still relatively limited by the fact that there are few Indians with expertise or training in international law.

We must also recognize that norm-setting at the international level is now happening at many different levels. Norm-setting is increasingly being determined not just by formal institutions like the UN, but also by informal associations and networks, particularly in fast-changing economic and technology sectors. NGOs are also increasingly important in norm creation at an international level and in mobilizing public opinion. It is also the case that the creation of international regulatory norms in one area can have profound implications for our strategic choices in other areas. This overall picture has to be kept in mind.

India is often accused of not participating in the creation of international norms and of free riding on the current system. This is a debatable subject. We have to recognize that often it can amount to a tactic to pressure India to do the Western powers' bidding. India must not be shy of projecting its own track record on norm creation. Part of this may be an issue of diplomatic projection. It is often more effective and accurate to say 'yes, but . . .' than an outright 'no'.

This is not merely a rhetorical point. Take the example of new norms on the international agenda like Responsibility to Protect or Democracy Promotion. Our commitment to important values like human rights, democracy and prevention of genocide must be very clear. And we should not be shy of projecting the fact that when we judged the circumstances to be right, and the instruments clearly defined, we have acted with full commitment on behalf of these values. India's intervention in 1971, for instance, is one of the most successful cases of intervention on behalf of human rights—and well before current doctrines of Responsibility to Protect. But at the same time we need to make it clear to the international community that the circumstances under which armed intervention is warranted on behalf of these values needs to be very carefully weighed, and that universal norms and values cannot provide a fig leaf for the pursuit of great power interests.

CHAPTER 3

Hard Power

India's foreign and strategic policy should aim at using a variety of tools, including diplomacy and deterrence, to prevent the outbreak of armed conflict. Nevertheless, a prudent state must consider various possible scenarios, where diplomacy and deterrence may fail, and armed conflict becomes inevitable. This chapter on hard power looks at these possible scenarios, given India's unique security environment. India's military doctrine remains defensive and the set of recommendations are in the nature of considered responses to acts of aggression.

India's hard power has as its instrumentalities the armed forces under the Ministry of Defence, the paramilitary forces and the Central Armed Police Forces under the Ministry of Home Affairs, and the state police under the respective state governments. The armed forces constitute one of the instruments that deal with external threats while internal threats are dealt with primarily by forces under the home ministry and state governments. Their main political objective and purpose is to ensure the creation of a stable and peaceful environment in order to facilitate maximum economic development concurrent with equitable growth. The political objective demands a peaceful international environment especially in our strategic neighbourhood that comprises the Asian land mass and the Indian Ocean littoral. The political objective also demands internal, political, social and economic stability. The role of hard power as an instrument of state is to remain ready to be applied externally or internally in pursuit of political objectives. Historically, the greatest threat to India is the combination of external threats during a period of internal instability.

External Challenges

The realm of external challenges requires hard power in the form of military power. These include, primarily, maintaining India's territorial integrity which encompasses land, sea and airspace frontiers. It also includes, among other things, the protection of trade routes, access to resources and protection of the Indian diaspora. Considering the unresolved disputes with China and Pakistan, India's borders with both these countries continue to remain politically deadlocked, curtailing free movement of people and trade. Continuing boundary disputes and other potential political issues mean that there is also the threat of war that demands military preparations. Towards the east, attempts to connect India to South-East Asia through India's Look East Policy have promise but still await fulfilment. In practice, the only direction in which India has greater freedom of projection is towards the Indian Ocean. Therefore the fundamental design that must underpin the shaping of India's military power should be the leveraging of potential opportunities that flow from peninsular India's location in the Indian Ocean, while concomitantly defending its land borders against Pakistan and China. The development of military power must therefore attain a significant maritime orientation. Presently, Indian military power has a continental orientation. To emerge as a maritime power should therefore be India's strategic objective.

That both China and Pakistan are nuclear armed directly impacts the type of wars that can be fought. India has propounded the concept of conventional space being available under a nuclear overhang. But the limitations of conventional space significantly diminish the scope of achievable political objectives. The major factor that influences the constriction of political objectives is the danger of escalation of war into the nuclear realm. Escalation is structurally intrinsic to war and is unpredictable as it involves an action and reaction chain between two independent wills. The decision to embark on war therefore will be weighed by the degree of risk that the political decision-maker is willing to take, and will depend on the issues at stake.

Beyond local border skirmishes, armed conflict will necessarily involve air power. Air power application in any war will first seek to neutralize the air assets of the adversary. It is aimed to achieve as much freedom for one's own aircraft to operate without interference, as also to minimize the adversary's ability to apply air power against one's own assets. This process cannot be confined to a limited geographical area and could encompass airfields, aircraft and air defence systems, among other targets. The geographical spread of the conflict is therefore difficult to contain. Escalation can also be inadvertent due to political signals and military actions being misinterpreted in the fog of war. Dual-use assets complicate the danger of escalation as it is not possible to distinguish a conventional armed aircraft or missile from a nuclear one. Consequently, nuclear weapons constrict the traditional utility of military force and call for a redefinition of our notions of 'victory'. The challenge for the military establishment is to shape our hard power capabilities in tandem with India's political objectives, while remaining within the ambit of the political and strategic logic imposed by nuclear weapons.

The shift to developing India's maritime power is possible if we align the shaping of our hard power with the political objectives feasible under a nuclear overhang. The window of opportunity is available, as Pakistan is likely to be enmeshed in internal strife and the Afghanistan imbroglio for the next decade or so. China is likely to remain focused on creating an environment that will facilitate the maintenance of its economic growth and internal stability. While Pakistan is preoccupied, India can make the shift by transforming its hard power capability in coherence with its political objectives. This should facilitate some shift of resources from the Pakistan border and building its defensive capability along the Sino-Indian border. Concurrently, resources can be allocated to develop its maritime capability and undertake a maritime shift in military power. This would also call for concomitant investment and development to enlarge our space assets, given that militaries are increasingly dependent on space assets for effective combat capability.

Pakistan

Capture of significant amounts of Pakistan's territory continues to be the primary military objective underpinning the doctrine and organization of the Indian armed forces. However, the capture of significant amounts of territory is no longer a valid proposition, owing to the nuclear equation. Also, except for the desert areas bordering Rajasthan and Gujarat, the density of population poses a danger of triggering humanitarian crises that may dwarf the advantages of military thrusts. In Pakistan-occupied Kashmir and Pakistani Punjab, where extremism is rife, we could find ourselves ensnared in a costly counter-insurgency campaign. The potency of insurgencies has also increased due to the technological empowerment of small groups, which can inflict significant physical and psychological damage through acts of terrorism.

The hard power strategy adopted by us will have to cover the spectrum that includes sending a political signal through military means at the lower end (through cyber or precision air attack) to capture of territory considered feasible under nuclear conditions at the higher end. The important issue is to shape our capabilities so that we effectively expand the range of practical options available under the nuclear overhang. The context of the particular situation will determine the range of actions. At the high end of the spectrum of usable military power we will need to review our prevailing operational doctrine and structures. The capability that India should acquire is one that enables us to make shallow thrusts that are defensible in as many areas as feasible along the international border and the LoC. This will require significant restructuring of the India's strike capability.

At the lower end of the options spectrum is the employment of cyber and/or air power in a punitive mode. The use of air/cyber power has advantages over any land-based strategy: it could be swift, more precise and certainly more amenable to being coordinated with our diplomatic efforts. Compared to any land-based options, the use of air/cyber power will come across as more restrained. To be sure, such action could invite retaliatory response from Pakistan. It is essential therefore that our coercive strategy not only caters for offensive use of air/cyber power but also for a defensive role. The principal role for the military will be denying Pakistani forces any ingress into Indian territory and preparing for the possibility of wider escalation. The crucial choice here requires a decision to move away from the paradigm focused on capture of territory to a paradigm based on destructive ability. Destructive capability will include air power, missiles and long-range guns as the central vectors. This would entail restructuring and also spare resources that we could deploy against China and yet retain the capability to switch resources to the west.

China

A Sino-Indian armed conflict will also be fought under a nuclear overhang. Though both countries have a doctrine of 'No First Use', the nuclear factor can be expected to impose caution on political decision-makers on both sides. The stakes at issue will again determine the degree of risk in political calculations. Generally, the nuclear factor can be expected to limit the scale of conflict and impact the scope of feasible political objectives.

Our frontiers with China have been mostly stable for some years now. However, there is a possibility that in certain circumstances China could assert its territorial claims (especially in the Arunachal sector or Ladakh) by the use of force. China might resort to localized territorial grabs. The most likely areas for such bite-sized operations are those parts of the Line of Actual Control (LAC) where both sides have different notions of where the LAC actually runs. These places are known. We cannot also entirely dismiss the possibility of a major military offensive in

Arunachal Pradesh or Ladakh. But such an offensive will not come as a bolt from the blue—there will be some warning in terms of an overall deterioration of diplomatic ties and significant military preparation by the Chinese as long as we have sufficient and reliable surveillance and intelligence capability.

In either case—whether China resorts to a limited probe or to a larger offensive—our aim should be the restoration of status quo ante. But this does not mean that we will have to resort to a purely defensive strategy. Indeed, given that the combat ratio and logistic networks favour China and that the attacker will always have the advantage of tactical (if not strategic) surprise, we will need a mix of defensive and offensive capabilities that can leverage the advantages that the terrain offers. Here again, we need to be clear about what kinds of offensive capabilities will be useful. The prevailing assumption that we should raise and deploy a 'mountain strike corps' against China is problematic. For it simply risks replicating all the problems with our existing strike corps under worse geographic and logistic conditions.

A more effective military doctrine would involve responding to limited land-grabs by China by undertaking similar action across the LAC: a strategy of quid pro quo. There are several areas where the local tactical and operational advantage rests with us. These areas should be identified and earmarked for limited offensive operations on our part. More important, such a strategy will need the creation of infrastructure for mobility and housing troops. It would also entail building up our existing defensive formations. But this could be done as part of a larger rationalization of force structure by transferring some forces that are currently deployed for operations against Pakistan. Though border infrastructure is under development, its progress has been slack and requires a major boost to speed up its implementation. Such a strategy will not only wrest the initiative from the Chinese, but will also be useful for our diplomatic efforts to restore status quo ante.

In the event of a major offensive by China, we cannot resort to a strategy of proportionate response. Rather we should look to leverage our asymmetric capabilities to convince the Chinese to back down. Three broad capabilities will be required to do so. First, we must be able to immediately trigger an effective insurgency in the areas occupied by Chinese forces. This would require careful preparation in advance. Special Forces could orchestrate the campaign. We also need to induct locals into paramilitary units and train them to switch to the guerrilla mode when required. We must acquire intelligence of all logistic and supply routes from Tibet into the occupied areas. Concurrently, we must develop the capability to interdict China's logistics and operational infrastructure in Tibet. We also need to earmark locations from which the insurgency will be operationally and logistically supported. All of these, it bears emphasizing, will require preparation well in advance. The fork in the road we need to choose is the politico-military strategy of quid pro quo and asymmetry as a means to defend our borders with China.

The second prong of our asymmetric strategy is to accelerate the integration of the frontier regions and its people by speeding up and improving communication infrastructure with the mainland. The third prong of our asymmetric strategy would have to be naval. We should be in a position to dominate the Indian Ocean region. The details of such operational capabilities are well understood. But it is worth emphasizing that such capability will require the development of our naval bases in the offshore island chains (especially the Andaman and Nicobar Islands) and of amphibious capabilities. The latter will require specialized and dedicated amphibious forces. Concurrent with the development of our naval capabilities should be a major thrust to exploit the potential of our exclusive economic zone in the Indian Ocean. Ocean development would not only include exploitation of the ocean resources but also the development of the infrastructure of our ports, connectivity to the hinterland, shipbuilding and ship repair capability, among other things. Due to the multiplicity of the agencies involved, there is need to establish a maritime commission. The crucial decision we face here concerns the quantum of additional resources that we must devote for developing our maritime power.

Border Management

India's extensive land and maritime borders pose significant challenges to India's national security. The system for prevention of illegal movement and maintaining the integrity of India's borders needs to be reviewed to increase its effectiveness. Presently, the maritime borders are jointly guarded by the Indian Coast Guard, navy and elements of the coastal state governments. A new system has been put in place consequent to the lessons learnt from the Mumbai attacks in 2008, but it is too early to comment on its efficacy. A constant review is, however, called for to minimize the dual responsibilities. The land borders are essentially guarded by the Central Armed Police Forces and paramilitary forces during peacetime, except for the Line of Control in Jammu and Kashmir and some portions of the Line of Actual Control on the Sino-Indian border, which are guarded by the army. Considering the sensitivity of the Sino-Indian border, there is a need to improve the integration between the Indo-Tibetan Border Police (ITBP) and the army. This is required because the Sino-Indian border, unlike most other land borders, is characterized not by illegal movement of peoples but instead is often subjected to transgressions. Therefore the present arrangement of two forces (ITBP and the army), each operationally under different ministries, does not lend itself easily towards integrated functioning. The way forward will require streamlining the operational command and control arrangements especially during peace.

Structural Changes

Dealing with the challenges presented by Pakistan and China requires several crucial changes to our defence and security structures. First, we should establish a maritime commission that will guide the development of India's maritime capabilities, and which should include ocean development, coastal infrastructure, shipping industry and naval capability. Second, we need to increase functional efficiency and improve civil–military relations, and this will require the establishment of an integrated Ministry of Defence by populating the ministry with civilian and armed forces personnel. We need to break with the present structure, based on an integrated defence staff that attempts to integrate only the service elements and actually acts as an additional layer between the individual services and a civilian Ministry of Defence. A Chairman Joint Chiefs of Staff should head the existing Integrated Defence Staff, which should become the Military Department of the Ministry of Defence. Third, we should establish integrated commands. These integrated commands will be organized operationally as integrated regional commands. Some integrated commands would be organized on a functional basis that could include Special Forces, air defence and logistics, among others. Fourth, the regional commanders should report to a Chairman Joint Chiefs of Staff, who will be supported by the Military Department. The pressing choice here is the decision to embark on a road map of structural changes commencing with the creation of the post of Chairman Joint Chiefs of Staff. While the arguments in favour of such restructuring and greater integration have been in the air for some time and have been broadly accepted, little in practice has been done in this regard. Given the type of potential threats India faces, this now needs urgent action. The restructuring of India's hard power must be animated by the idea of aligning it with envisaged political objectives.

CHAPTER 4

Internal Security

India contains many potential sources of conflict, and a variety of causes that can serve to activate these potentials at different times. Economic and material interests are one such source, while claims to recognition of identities, whether social or cultural, are another recurring one. The causes that incite conflicts can range from slow processes of historical awakening among groups, leading to the valid assertion of rights, to sudden contingencies that can inflame once-calm parts of the country. The crucial point from a strategic perspective, however, is that the particular forms in which conflicts, whether deep-set or newborn, manifest themselves are heavily dependent on the political skills through which they are handled. How a group of people chooses to engage with the state—whether by violent protest, by civil dissent or by electoral participation—is a matter which is very much in the hands of political elites, of the elected leaders and state managers, and their would-be challengers. It is important to insist therefore that how conflicts are articulated, and in particular whether or not they reach a point where they threaten India's internal security, is a direct consequence of political actions and agency. There is nothing predetermined or inevitable about how these conflicts develop, no matter how deep-set their structural causes may be. Politics matters, and from a strategic point of view a primary goal must be to foster the political judgement and skills required to contain and minimize such conflicts—and to make them amenable to political solutions.

Politics indeed matters. Failure to recognize that, and the implications it carries for a strategic perspective on internal security matters, results in haphazard adoption of uneven policies, pursued in ad hoc ways, as supposed remedies for the root causes of conflict. So, whether it be Naxalism or ethnic conflict, there is a standard toolkit for addressing root causes that is invariably articulated: investing in development, providing social services, lifting a sense of siege, or in some cases overcoming geographical isolation, providing cultural protection, and so forth. The list is often unexceptionable, and not difficult to conjure up. But what is harder to diagnose is why this wish list is difficult to implement even by well-meaning governments, and why so little is affected by it. A strategic approach needs to proceed not by proliferating more 'need-to-do lists', but by identifying the main existing and coming sources of conflict (while recognizing of course the always present surprise factor: there are, from time to time, quite new and unexpected conflicts that emerge), and creating political conditions for defusing in advance such conflicts. India has plenty of experience in the more or less effective management of conflict; but a strategic vision must have conflict prevention as its goal.

A full analysis of the challenges of internal security is beyond the scope of this document. It is widely recognized that if internal security challenges proliferate, India's global prospects are diminished in many ways. The viability and prestige of our developmental model is diminished. The potential of outside powers exploiting internal fissures increases. The allocation of resources required to deal with internal conflicts inflicts a huge opportunity cost. And we are less authoritatively able to take moral leadership on a global stage. Internal security should therefore be as much an object of all-party consensus as external relations.

While operational aspects are beyond the scope of this document, a few general points ought to be kept in mind when thinking of internal security. Internal security challenges are largely exacerbated by three kinds of state failures. The Indian state has the capacity to address these failures. But our failure to address them speaks poorly of our commitment to internal security.

The first failure is state abdication. In significant parts of the country, the state has simply abdicated its role in providing basic services and vacated the space for all kinds of groups to acquire control. Examples of state abdication include the absence of effective civilian administration in several tribal areas. But they also include absence of effective justice systems in some urban areas. Various armed groups step into this vacuum to effectively provide a parallel, if predatory, government. Once these groups take control of the local political economy, it is difficult to dislodge them. The strengthening of all aspects of routine civilian administration, and giving the state an effective presence, must be top priority. So much of our recent discourse on the state has been about taking the state out of particular domains. We have neglected to ask where we need to bring the state back in.

The second failure is the state as predator. We need to openly acknowledge this blunt truth. In many parts of the country, the state has a history of a protracted and brutal suppression of violence, and of abuses of human rights. Often this is not because the state is ill-intentioned but because it is weak, and compensates for weakness by acting with impunity. In many parts of India, the law and order machinery is considered a source of *insecurity*. Often the sense of insecurity produced by the state leads to a vicious circle: repressive measures by the state lead to more alienation, and invite greater repression in turn. It is in this context that human rights are important. Protecting human rights is not an antithesis of security; it is one of its preconditions. The state needs to strengthen its protection of human rights, even—indeed, above all—in conflict-ridden areas.

The third state failure is the state's failure to be impartial. The Indian Constitution's moral promise is that no citizen will be targeted for their identity. The Indian state has often failed to live up to this promise. Whatever may be the reality, the *fear* that the state is partial to one community or the other is a source of alienation. The sense that the machinery of the state is partial is reflected principally in two domains: policing and politics. There is a perception that Indian policing is very much inflected by considerations of identity. These considerations sometimes lead it to come to premature judgements about which individuals or groups pose a threat. In politics, our failure stems from the fact that there is almost no investigation of major events like communal riots or encounter killings that are not subject to political controversy. The state is often unable to project the idea that it can be credibly impartial. Some parts of the state—perhaps the judiciary—are able to do it more than others. But if the state cannot credibly project impartiality in its investigations, prosecution and justice, it will remain at risk internally.

The republic's large scale has been an advantage for us, since it makes it very difficult for any single ethnic group to seriously challenge the state in ways that fundamentally jeopardize the state's survival. Since challenging a large state is difficult, this often reduces incentives to engage in state-subverting secessionism. It does not, though, eradicate them entirely: and such incentives can become attractive when the state is itself perceived as posing a threat to a particular region or group. But success, based on our sheer size, must not make us complacent.

In the long run, the greatest hope for dealing with internal security problems remains the strength of our democracy. So long as citizens have the belief that they are genuinely being heard, the incentives to violence will come down. In fact, all the historical evidence makes clear that secessionist movements that aim to subvert the state tend to arise—or become more virulent—when central governments have themselves weakened democratic provisions and have adopted more centralizing or even authoritarian forms of conduct. Secessionist movements in Punjab, Kashmir and the North-East have each in equal measure drawn sustenance from local perceptions of the Centre's meddling and authoritarianism. On the other hand, whenever the state has respected the federal spirit and principles and tried genuine democratic incorporation, it has more often than not succeeded. The best strategy to achieve internal security thus remains a commitment to practices and procedures of democratic incorporation of all citizens via the federal architecture. In this context, both human rights and political and civil liberties cannot be seen as discretionary grants from the political authorities, or as optional values that can be rescinded in pursuit of internal security. They have to be the bedrock of our federal democracy.

It is important to remember that as much as the formal guarantees embodied in the Constitution and in legislation, it is informal mechanisms of working together—what one might call a 'culture of federalism'—that can sustain incorporation and make diversity one of India's distinctive strengths. Purely constitutionalist approaches will not have much effect unless they are followed in the context of political processes premised on the experience of working together.

Politics—in the sense of the informal practices of negotiation—have been important to India's success as a democracy. But politics more broadly can sometimes exacerbate conflict through a number of mechanisms. First, in many instances, rather than objective circumstances, it was in fact politics—judgements and choices on the part of leaderships, both national and local—that transformed movements of political dissent into a crisis that threatened the state. The role of 'political entrepreneurship' in fostering grievance without significant root cause, or by misdiagnosing the cause, must not be underestimated. Second, the state's misjudgements about the use of force, at times employing too little, at times too much, become a crucial variable in escalating conflict. But these judgements are often hostage to political considerations. Third, politics that takes into account identities of citizens is inevitable in a country like India. Often this is necessary because identity can be the axis around which injustice is structured. But politics can sometimes create the conditions for competitive communalism by generating a sense of insecurity in one community or the other.

India needs to have faith in the power of its democracy. There is absolutely no doubt that India faces risks of home-grown terrorism in several communities and regions. These need to be dealt with through appropriate and effective security measures. But the important thing to remember is that the fringes in any community can grow more extreme even as the mainstream is moderating. The challenge is to cut off political support for the fringes.

The North-East and Kashmir pose a special challenge for a number of reasons. First, the absence of cross-cutting elite penetration between state-level politicians and the Centre makes political management difficult. Second, these regions are, at least in principle, examples of 'asymmetric' federalism. Many of these states had, ironically, stronger protections of their special status and identities than other states (for example, restrictions on immigration in many states of the North-East and Kashmir). Third, the transnational dimension to conflict is significant and plays out differently. Fourth, the central state has had a more protracted and brutal history of suppression of violence, suspension of democracy and humans rights abuses in these two regions. Indeed, these regions have been subject to very ambivalent treatment by the Indian state, which has been simultaneously very accommodating and repressive, producing what might, in Machiavelli's words, be called a state that is neither feared nor loved.

The North-East itself is a highly differentiated region: the problems of Assam have very different social roots as compared with Manipur. In many other areas of the country, the alignment of territoriality and ethnicity could provide a basis for resolving demands. Not so, though, in the North-East, where attempts to align territoriality and ethnicity only functioned to generate more demands. Once the dominant framework became territoriality, it led to more conflicts because it made minorities in each potential state insecure; it led to conflicting claims over territoriality; and it gave a greater incentive to mobilize around territorial self-determination. The region thus remained entrapped in conflicting territorial claims. The simple truth is that no territorially based solutions alone are likely to work in the North-East. Alternatives that were suggested included mechanisms like non-territorially based representation in the assemblies of particular states and the guarantee of cultural and linguistic rights. It was felt that the structures of representation needed to move away from a fixation with territoriality, in order to facilitate accommodation of various competing interests. For instance, it will not be possible to redraw substantially the boundaries of a given state without risking more unrest from other groups. The alignment of territoriality and representation may not always work. The terms in which inclusive governance is achieved need to be changed.

There has been no shortage of analysis of the policy measures that need to be undertaken to 'restore' the North-East. The region has long been a 'frontier' zone, tenuously attached to the Indian 'mainland' and with sensitive international borders: all of which have made it subject to the security imperatives of the Indian state. This has created a sense of siege in the North-East. The region needs access to traditional trade routes, opening of transport corridors and in general improvement of connectivity with other parts of India as well as the regional neighbourhood. This is a worthwhile objective, for altered patterns of trade have the potential to lift the sense of siege and change the local political economy. But we need to ask the conditions under which such measures are likely to succeed or even be attempted.

In almost every conflict zone, 'development' itself has not been able to bypass or dismantle existing structures of violence. It has sometimes fed into them. To prescribe development as a remedy for the North-East is an analytically blunt assessment. The institutional architecture that delivers development will be vital.

Migration, from within, but also from outside India's borders, is a considerable source of conflict, putting immense pressure on land and jobs. In many ways, migrants are now an integral part of the economy of the North-East, and in the new economy much more labour is coming in. While migrants had become an integral part of the economy, their political rights and status could not officially be acknowledged because many were considered illegal. The state's approach to managing illegal migration has been largely to see it as a problem of policing: based on the hope that more border fences, border guards and periodic hunts would deter migrants. But the fundamental fact is that the economy and ecology of the North-East is deeply intertwined with that of Bangladesh, and both the demand- and the supply-side factors (for example, lack of economic opportunities in the border areas of Bangladesh) make it unlikely that migration will stop any time soon.

It is, therefore, time to think creatively about managing this migration. Instead of operating with unsustainable categories like citizen and non-citizen, it would be desirable to introduce a system of work permits that would more frankly acknowledge the realities on the ground, would allow migration to be documented and managed better, but would still preserve the sense that there is a distinction between citizens and people who come here for work. It would protect the rights of both groups better.

The other blunt truth is that the Central government will have to take some political risk. Apart from the burden of past wrongs, which the state has yet to recognize, the single most potent symbol of alienation in the North-East remains the Armed Forces (Special Powers) Act.

Despite a concerted campaign over the last five years and promises made from the highest levels, this act is no closer to being repealed than it was several years ago. Nor has any effort been made to give citizens a credible assurance that grievance redressal mechanisms will be made more effective. The AFSPA has therefore become a symbol of permanent political estrangement. The problems posed by it need to be addressed.

A better understanding of political discourse among various groups in the region is also needed. They remain trapped in negotiating impasses. There are two big obstacles to creating new political discourses. First, leaders fear becoming hostage to the logic of radicalism noted above, which seeks to succeed by outbidding. Often this makes them vulnerable to violence from within. A state needs a political strategy to defuse this threat—and political leaders who are willing to take the risk. Without addressing this issue, no conflict can be resolved. Second, almost all the measures states propose to alleviate grievances, like development, opening the economy and infrastructure, do not address political narratives around identity or political grievances linked to rights abuses. The great resilience of territorial demands and demands for representation and justice is that they tap into a collective politics of self-esteem. Development can provide resources and escape mechanisms to individuals. This is important, but it needs to be accompanied by a narrative that replaces the romance of identity politics with a new narrative of integration and economic advancement. There are few examples of politicians who have been able to convert a narrative of identity, resentment and fear into a narrative of hope and change.

In addition to continuing regional state-level conflicts, the Indian state will face two types of new challenges of inclusive governance: sub-regional demands and conflicts over megacities. The Telangana movement exemplifies the challenge of sub-state nationalism, and a couple of general lessons emerge from it. First, there is no objective basis for determining the optimal size of states. While an intuitive case can be made that several of India's states are too big to provide accessible governance, what counts as an optimal or viable state does not lend itself to delineation in terms of necessary and sufficient conditions. What is evident is large intra-state inequalities in India's states. Ideally these can be addressed through normal policy instruments. But increasingly—sometimes even without justification—intra-state inequality will be attributed by those subject to its effects to active discrimination by the state, rather than being seen as a product of complex economic processes. In this sense, intra-state inequality poses a political challenge. When intra-state inequality is cast as a political challenge, the 'bring development' slogan may not be sufficient: the state may have to concede, in the name of development, the demands of poorer regions, as it did in 2000. Yet the conundrum is that once it deeply legitimizes the principle of sub-regional nationalism, it could have cascade effects, as happened in the North-East. There are, in principle, other solutions—which can lie anywhere between the formation of new states to the creation of local government. One might also experiment with intermediate structures like regional boards, such as the Ladakh Hill Council, for instance. These regional representative structures have been often put on paper and talked about, but seldom implemented.

The second big emerging challenge for inclusive governance centres on India's most successful cities: What is the place of megacities, both in defining India's global profile and in domestic political equations? The fact is that mega cities like Hyderabad and Mumbai are sources of immense economic power. The great conflict is over the resources these cities provide. Even in Telangana, part of the ambition is to diminish the alleged control of outsiders over the resources of Hyderabad. States like Uttar Pradesh, where there is no dominant urban centre, will be easier to divide into smaller states; but states like

Maharashtra, Andhra Pradesh and Karnataka, which possess high-stake urban centres, may find themselves embroiled in protracted conflicts which could paralyse their productive centres. India simply does not have a framework for megacity governance. But these cities are increasingly going to be at once the sites and objects of conflict: questions centring on who controls their vast resources, who is allowed into these cities, and others will become pressing. From a strategic point of view, we will need to evolve frameworks of state, local and urban government that can enable the governance needs of megacities, fostering their economic dynamism and cosmopolitan identities.

We also have to acknowledge that there are certain sectors of the citizenry for which the state has failed to provide a viable place in the federal architecture. Adivasis are the truly marginalized citizens of India's federal democracy. Confined to areas where the state has had a fitful and arbitrary presence, few of their promised rights as citizens have been delivered to them. Further, they have seen their traditional forms and sources of livelihood collapse around them, without being provided the tools to enter into the more modern sectors of the economy. Finally, unlike other hitherto marginalized groups like the Dalits, the Adivasis have no overarching emancipatory narrative, no effective mainstream party and political leadership, and no capacity to mobilize in politically significant ways within established structures.

Part of the difficulty with Adivasi policy has been its construction around a fundamentally flawed dichotomy. For a long time, the state and planners have seen the choices before them as either one of promoting the gradual integration and access of Adivasis to the wider economy or of creating enclaves where traditional ways of life can, to a certain degree, be preserved. What this dichotomy between 'assimilation' and arcadia obscures is the fact that 'integration' with the wider economy has always been on terms that have been unfavourable to the Adivasis, who lose their land and homes for large projects without getting in exchange tangible, long-term benefits out of them. Add the ecological factor, and it is clear that the cost society carries for this sort of 'integration' is greater than the sum of individual costs the Adivasis themselves bear. Finding ways of harnessing the economic potential of Adivasi lands in a manner that sustains and eventually enriches the environment as well as Adivasi lives is the principal challenge facing the Indian state.

Another segment of the citizenry that has fallen through the interstices of the federal architecture are those very diverse groups that are clubbed together under the heading

135

of Left Wing Extremism (LWE) and Naxalites: loose terms, of course, since there is considerable variation across them in terms of ideology, organization, strategy and local political opportunities. A full analysis of the Naxal movement is beyond the scope of this document. But some analytical observations are germane to the strategic perspective with which we are concerned. First, Naxalism too—like every one of the forms of conflict we have noted in this chapter—is a primarily political form of struggle and conflict. No doubt it feeds on objective background conditions: landlessness, deprivation and alienation. But it is articulated into a specific form of armed revolutionary ideology as a result of politics.

Although there is a family resemblance between different Naxal groups, their tactics and political viability depend largely on local conditions—which even in their core areas show great variance. Andhra Pradesh, for instance, had experienced great Naxal violence till early 2000, but then managed to bring it under control. In Bihar, all the data show that Naxal violence has varied considerably across districts, almost disappearing for years on end. The same is true of West Bengal. In most of these instances, the state decided to intervene in various ways, usually a combination of coercion and development. The interesting question is: What determines the state's resolve to intervene? The Indian state is quite capable of controlling violence if it so desires: suppression of insurgency has historically been one of the state's strengths. So why is there such enormous variation in the state's response? Where does politics have a role in this?

The standard response of the state in combating Naxalism is through a combination of 'law and order' approaches and development. There are two crucial questions on the law and order front. On the one hand, in a federal system, interstate coordination between police forces is very weak. Indeed, there is evidence that Naxals do a form of forum shopping, escaping from states that are taking concerted action into bordering districts of other states. The very success of anti-Naxal operations in some areas can produce more violence in others. A challenge for federal systems is whether policing of this kind should be a local function—or should it have a more centralized dimension? On the other hand, even where there are 'unified commands', success has continued to prove elusive.

The state often relies on counter-insurgency operations. These are successful to varying degrees, though often at terrible human cost. But a common thread running through conflict management in India is that there is still no serious attempt at making the presence of the state more effective in its routine policing functions. One of the big political economy puzzles is: Why do states not invest more resources and institutional energy in police reform? The politics of Naxalism is crucially linked to this larger question. There is a real danger that even where counter-insurgency operations are successful, the state will not invest in creating routine policing functions. In developing country democracies, police reforms are the lowest priority item. Again, almost every single report on Naxalism talks about strengthening civilian administration. But there is little effective pressure to bring about the necessary reforms in either of these domains.

In some respects, it will be the failure of the state, if it needs to resort to hard power for domestic security. The emphasis should be on preventive measures and political solutions, including, eventually, negotiations and peace talks. But in the eventuality that hard power has to be used domestically, it needs some restructuring.

Insofar as hard power is concerned, the most important capability would be locally raised and well-trained police forces operating responsibly and with a degree of accountability—without the culture of impunity which has often led to large-scale rights violations and generally exacerbated the conflict. The current pattern of relying on Central paramilitary forces to compensate for the weaknesses of state police units is problematic. The Central paramilitaries tend to lack the necessary knowledge of local geography, language and customs. Besides, their training for such operations leaves a lot to be desired in terms of tactical skills and soft skills required to win over the local population. Given the range and location of the Maoist insurgency (and its potential for spreading out), relying on the paramilitaries or the army would be unrealistic. The states must raise, equip and field police forces that are embedded in local conditions. But it cannot abdicate its responsibilities to citizens' militias or vigilante groups, as Chhattisgarh's use of the Salwa Judum has shown. The Central government must help states devise proper recruitment and training procedures. In particular, these must equip local recruits with all the capabilities and knowledge necessary for effective policing. The army too could play a larger role in training such forces. We need to focus on strengthening the state police forces vis-á-vis the Central Armed Police/paramilitary forces. But in the end there is no substitute for building effective states.

The Central Armed Police Forces comprise slightly less than two million personnel. The armed forces comprise nearly 1.2 million. With the requirement to keep the armed forces young, there is a need to establish a flow of personnel from the armed forces to the Central Armed Police Forces and vice versa. This will have two major spin-offs. First, it will reduce the burgeoning pension bill of the armed forces substantially. Second, it will facilitate transfer of skills from the armed forces to the Central Armed Police Forces. Though the need for such a manpower policy has been recognized, its implementation has not been possible due to institutional turf battles, and achieving this will require political direction and guidance.

The operational complexities are numerous, and our discussion in this chapter is not even a remotely adequate acknowledgement of these complexities. But there has to be a consensus on three things if India is to avoid continued and serious internal conflict. First, we need to build a credible state that makes citizens feel secure. Second, we need to further develop models of inclusive governance that can address the sense of disempowerment in certain sections of the population. Third, we need a political culture that is attuned to defusing conflict rather than exacerbating it.

CHAPTER 5

Non-conventional Security Issues

Energy Security

A significant constraint on India's ability to reach and maintain 8 to 10 per cent growth over the next several decades, and to take advantage of the so-called 'demographic dividend', will be the availability of energy resources. India's strategic autonomy will depend profoundly on its energy policy. The more dependent it is on imported fossil fuels or technology, the less autonomy will it have. Indeed, more than anything else, energy dependence often defines the limits of power. Energy competition is likely to remain an important driver of strategic competition.

Our energy security situation puts us in a position of structural dependence. Our dependence on imported oil is already 75 per cent and is estimated to go up to 90 per cent by 2030–31. Most of the oil is sourced from potentially volatile regions such as the Gulf. While the situation concerning natural gas is better, the rising curve of demand will result in a steep rise in imports by 2030–31. There is an urgent need to assess and exploit shale gas deposits on India's continental shelf. Thanks to shale gas, the United States is virtually self-sufficient in natural gas—though it was a major importer only a few years ago. However, a number of environmental issues, in particular water contamination, have arisen with shale gas production and need careful examination. In particular, India's regulatory capacities may need substantial enhancement before we attempt sustainable shale gas production. Above all, we should not arrive at a situation where solving one resource crunch leads to a more problematic situation in another more critical resource, that is, water.

Coal is likely to remain the mainstay of India's power generation. Over 50 per cent of current commercial energy is sourced to coal and this is unlikely to change in the short to medium term. It is estimated that 66 to 75 per cent of coal in 2030–31 would be imported. This appears to be based on a pessimistic analysis of the existing coal industry in India. This in turn points to the need for denationalization of coal and for reform of Coal India Limited and of the overall sector as a security imperative. The recent Committee on Allocation of Natural Resources offers a graduated path for such reform. Further, even if

144

this level of import continues, there are severe constraints in port capacity for such import volumes (we have few specialized coal terminals) and associated logistics of evacuation from the port to sites of use.

Hydroelectric power is about 20 per cent of our current power production, but is unlikely to rise in any significant manner, particularly due to environmental constraints. These constraints exist for almost all sources, particularly for coal but also for non-fossil sources like wind and nuclear energy. Further, hydroelectric power needs to be repositioned as primarily a supplier of peak power, which may require reconfiguration of the plants at the sites to produce more electricity within a shorter time frame, that is, more turbines.

Nuclear energy constitutes only 3 per cent of our current power production and may rise to 10 per cent by 2030–31 if the projected expansion, in the wake of the Indo-US civil nuclear agreement, fructifies. In this effort, it is important to look at the experience of countries that have rapidly increased the share of electricity from nuclear power such as France and Japan and understand the kind of institutional oversight, regulatory architecture and execution capacity that needs to be created in the public and private sectors for enabling such scaling-up.

Overall, India's energy security is likely to deteriorate

in the short to medium term and the challenge will be to ensure predictable and adequate supplies from external sources, to ramp up energy-use efficiency at home and to remove constraints on expanding domestic supplies of all available sources of energy.

In the longer term, there is no alternative to making a strategic shift from our current reliance on fossil fuels to a pattern of production and consumption based, progressively, on renewable and clean sources of energy (such as nuclear energy). There will have to be a conscious effort to move away from energy- and resource-intensive patterns of growth to a model that is energy-conserving, which focuses on developing more public goods rather than focusing on individual consumption, for instance promoting cheap and efficient public transportation as against private vehicular traffic. The impact of such a shift will be felt in the longer term. But critical decisions to bring this about have to be taken now.

India is at a stage of growth where creation of infrastructure is a priority. It is also urbanizing rapidly. The choices we make now in terms of urban design and infrastructure development will constrain our possibilities for years to come. So energy efficiency and the technology and resource choices needed to achieve such efficiency must be placed at the centre of such decisions.

It is true that India has managed many of the demand-side issues well. The energy intensity of organized industry has been improving. India taxes all kinds of fuels. But this poses a strategic challenge for us. For, on the one hand, it signals a certain capacity to respond to energy concerns. On the other, it suggests that our headroom for making improvements is much less than many of our competitors.

There is an urgent need to align our plans for augmenting power-generation capacity with emerging demand patterns. Current indications are that virtually all the planned additional capacity is in the nature of base load capacity, with very little available to cater to peak load demand. We need the right mix to cater both to base load and to peak load demand. Our current mix is suboptimal. It is projected that power demand for space conditioning (which creates both diurnal and seasonal variations in demand) will be the fastest-growing component of energy use in the next twenty to thirty years. Therefore in terms of energy strategy:

a. There must be focus on power-generation capacity to meet load—following demand and peak demand, rather than base load.

b. Demand-side management will require introduction of time-of-day tariffs and a power distribution system responsive to demand variations.

c. We need to create a national and eventually subcontinental power grid network that enables more efficient energy use and the introduction of smart grid systems, which can integrate the use of emerging decentralized technologies like micro turbines (for uses that combine space conditioning and power) and fuel cells.

The Indian public and private sector oil companies are actively seeking energy sources abroad, from mines in Australia, Indonesia and Bolivia and oil exploration blocs in Central and South-East Asia, Russia, Africa and Latin America. These transactions are likely to pose new strategic challenges for Indian foreign policy. We need to establish the bargaining levers to ensure that these contracts work in India's favour, and do not draw the government into diplomatic compromises it might otherwise want to avoid. In this context, India must take into account the transformational impact of the shale gas revolution on the global energy landscape. The exploitation of vast reserves of shale gas in the United States using new technologies such as fracking and horizontal drilling, has already made it self-sufficient in gas and a potential major LNG exporter. Indian diplomacy must vigorously pursue an energy partnership with the United States, using its privileged relationship with that country, so that its energy security is advanced even as it continues its strategy of a graduated shift to renewable and clean sources of energy. This may also reduce India's dependence on energy supplies from an increasingly volatile West Asia and North Africa.

According to the Petroleum Conservation Research Association (PCRA), the consumption pattern of petroleum products in India is as follows:

Consumption Pattern of Petroleum Products in India (%)	
Transport (petrol, diesel, CNG, aviation fuel)	51
Domestic (LPG and kerosene)	18
Industry (petrol, diesel, fuel oil, naphtha, natural gas, largely for supplementary power generation and feedstock)	14
Commercial and Others	13
Agriculture (diesel)	4

The issue is not so much fossil fuels or technology; rather it is about choices that keep options open and those that compel lock-ins. For example, a system that is based largely on electricity (electric buses and cars for transport, electric cooking stoves, electric pumps instead of diesel pumps, with no necessity to continuously run backup generators in buildings and factories, electric trains, etc.) offers more options in terms of fuel sources, since electricity can be generated in a number of ways and using different sources. However, if the system depends on transport by liquid fuel, diesel pump sets, captive generation fuelled by diesel, diesel locomotives, and so on, then the options are obviously much more limited. As of now, even with current technologies, it seems feasible to aim at shifting localized personal passenger and freight transport, as well as much of public transport, to electricity. Long-range and heavy freight may require breakthrough technologies; but if one can limit liquid fuel use to largely these requirements, then considerable insulation can be achieved.

Energy security in this scenario would then be tied much more to the electrification of transport systems and homes and, more important, to the improvement in our electricity generation, transmission and distribution. A reliable electricity sector with sufficient capacity is thus a prime security concern.

The subsidiary implication of the focus on electrification would be to ensure that the production of electricity is sufficiently robust and sustainable in terms of fuel supplies. Coal and various forms of coal-related technologies—for example, an increase in the efficient use of Indian coal, in-situ coal gasification, coal to liquids (while this was uneconomical earlier when the price of liquid fuel was much lower, it can be commercially viable now; about a quarter of South Africa's liquid fuel needs are met from coal)—and the associated greenhouse gas implications, need to be placed more centrally on the agenda. Equally, the issue of the denationalization of the coal sector in order to permit a more vibrant local coal industry, instead of the current mix of various subsidiaries of Coal India Limited and connected private players, needs to be debated.

However, one must recognize that reliance on electricity can also be a limitation, as is evident in developed countries when natural disasters affect electricity supplies. Thus, a suitable backup emergency system would need to be put in place concomitant with electrification. Along with these actions on the supply side, there needs to be greater focus on demand-side actions. With electrification, this can be much more finely tuned, since the pricing can be much more dynamic and IT-based.

Nuclear Security and Options

The pursuit and maintenance of nuclear capability has been integral to India's quest for strategic autonomy since Independence. There has been a consensus among successive governments on this issue—even in the face of immense international pressure and sanctions. In the absence of a credible nuclear deterrent, India would have few options when confronted with adversaries possessing nuclear weapons.

The objective of India's nuclear policy is credible minimum deterrent. India has a stated nuclear doctrine with a declared no-first-use policy. It also has an exemplary record both on non-proliferation and on safeguarding its nuclear material. In contrast to the expectation of several observers and analysts, India has neither gone for unjustifiable expansion of its arsenal nor adopted a destabilizing nuclear posture.

But our nuclear policy has to be situated in the light of emerging, and often contradictory, realities of the global and regional environment. These realities will be a source of pressure on us from different directions. There are emerging trends to which we need to respond.

The continued growth and modernization of the Chinese and Pakistani nuclear arsenals should be a matter of some concern to India. In the context of the power transition and accompanying changes under way in the Asia-Pacific region, it is likely that the Chinese arsenal will expand. The range and sophistication of China's delivery systems are already increasing. This will have an implication for India's nuclear policy and strategy. Similarly, Pakistan's nuclear programme is set to expand in the foreseeable future. The cooperation between China and Pakistan on nuclear matters further complicates the situation for India.

As indicated in Chapter One, India will have to continue to deal with the consequences of a nuclear Pakistan. The presence of nuclear weapons has simultaneously emboldened Pakistan to pursue sub-conventional options against India and posed certain constraints on India's strategic response. Further, given the absence of a published nuclear doctrine for Pakistan and the deliberate cultivation of ambiguity on the part of Pakistan, the nuclear balance in the subcontinent is far from reassuring.

The sources of nuclear proliferation globally are likely to increase. At one level, we will see more states attempting to acquire nuclear weapons capability. This will be driven by a combination of the desire to obviate the possibility of external military intervention and of the imperatives stemming from regional rivalries. At another level, the reliance on nuclear power, notwithstanding the Fukushima accident, is likely to increase—at least outside Europe. The threat of nuclear terrorism will certainly be higher in this context—with nuclear facilities and plants themselves as targets.

There is greater global pressure for the 'Zero Nuclear Option'. Unlike the earlier calls for complete nuclear disarmament (in the mid-1950s and early 1980s), the current round of activism is spurred not by protests from below but by policy initiatives from above. Whilst the involvement of great power elites makes the process more promising, it also provokes scepticism: there is a danger that the global zero discourse may end up being merely the pursuit of traditional non-proliferation objectives by other means. After all, traditional nuclear powers, like the United States and Russia, still have 90 per cent of the world's nuclear arsenal and are in no hurry to reduce them significantly. Nor is China open to capping, let alone giving up, nuclear weapons any time soon. All the same, the global zero discourse will be a source of pressure on countries to forsake their nuclear ambitions. If not done in the context of global disarmament, such pressure could put countries like India, which have modest and less-tested arsenals, at a disadvantage.

India's response to this evolving situation and divergent imperatives needs to be underpinned by a set of strategic principles. To begin with, our nuclear policy should emphasize the hardening and survivability of our arsenal. In the face of the growing nuclear arsenals in our neighbourhood, we need to ensure an assured second-strike capability. Our main effort must be devoted to the development of the maritime leg of our nuclear capability and the accompanying command and control systems. We also need to work towards the operationalization of our missile defence capabilities. There will be external pressure to desist from this course, on the grounds that it will lead to a nuclear arms race in the region. We must forthrightly point out that such arguments are confusing the causes for the consequences.

Second, India should adopt a proactive stance against nuclear proliferation. We should be open to participating in international counter-proliferation initiatives that are non-discriminatory and are consonant with international law. Further, we should draw attention to the underlying drivers of insecurity that may be propelling certain states to acquire nuclear weapons and to the need to address these basic issues if non-proliferation is to succeed in the longer run.

Third, to prevent nuclear terrorism we need a combination of unilateral and multilateral measures. Deterring nuclear terrorism will require substantial upgrading of our screening and surveillance capabilities at various entry points along our land borders (especially those with Pakistan) as well as our air- and seaports. Then again, the current state of technology for screening nuclear material is not sufficiently advanced. We therefore need to adopt a clear declaratory policy on nuclear terrorism. Our stated nuclear doctrine needs to be amended to affirm the responsibility of the state from which nuclear weapons or material may be stolen. It should clarify that we will be willing to act on strong but less than perfect information. This would help disabuse any state of the notion that it can claim helplessness in preventing theft of material or warheads.

Given that the acquisition or development and use of a fully fashioned nuclear device by terrorist outfits is rather difficult, the most likely form of nuclear terrorism is the use of a 'dirty bomb'. The psychological and public effect of the detonation of a 'dirty bomb' will be enormous. But its physical effects, especially in terms of contamination, are likely to be relatively mild and capable of being contained—provided we have the necessary capabilities and expertise. We need urgently to look into this aspect of disaster management.

More important, we need to take steps to develop capacities for attribution and to strengthen capabilities in nuclear forensics. Any response to a nuclear attack carried out by a terrorist group will rest on our ability to identify the source (primarily inferred from the isotope). The best way forward would be to step up cooperation with the United States and other countries in nuclear forensics, and to invest in the enhancement of our own research and development (R&D) capabilities in this area.

Fourth, we should make it clear that complete nuclear disarmament is, and has always been, an objective of Indian policy. The history of India's tryst with nuclear weapons is ample testimony to this fact. At various points in the past decades, India has been in the forefront of efforts to promote nuclear disarmament. The Rajiv Gandhi plan of 1988 represents the most recent effort to convey a sincere and credible message to the world that nuclear disarmament needs to be taken seriously. That plan is currently being updated.

India should support the current calls for global zero, provided these are sincere, fair and non-discriminatory. We should also be prepared not to stand in the way of the Comprehensive Nuclear-Test-Ban Treaty (CTBT), provided all nuclear powers recognized by the Nuclear Non-Proliferation Treaty (NPT) are prepared to do so. At the same time, we should recognize that neither global zero nor CTBT may be attainable any time soon. We should direct our efforts at measures designed to delegitimize nuclear weapons. Till such time as nuclear weapons are accepted as currency of power in international politics, complete nuclear disarmament will remain a chimera.

Towards this end, we need to promote with greater seriousness and vigour a proposal that we have already mooted: a global no-first-use (NFU) treaty. This will go a considerable distance in reducing the strategic and psychological importance of nuclear weapons. If accomplished in tandem with deep cuts to their arsenals by the major nuclear powers, this could set the stage for serious efforts at the total elimination of nuclear weapons. By pushing for a global NFU treaty, we could credibly work to advance the cause of disarmament without prematurely compromising our own security.

CHAPTER 6

Knowledge and Information
Foundations

A nation needs to continually reinvent itself as it moves up the growth curve. Every doubling of its gross domestic product (GDP) puts the nation at the cusp of transformation for the next doubling. Simply put, there is much more at stake when the GDP per capita is $2000 as opposed to $200. People begin to have an expectation of the future, rather than to worry about survival. This expectation of a better future manifests itself in a number of ways, such as demands for accountable leadership, good governance, equal opportunity, security and asserting a place in the world. India's fundamental institutions will need to be transformed to meet these expectations, to keep up with the times and to keep up with growth. Failure to do so can lead to instability and thus become a risk to national security, whereas embracing such transformations can actually enhance national security.

Such transformations can be accelerated by focusing on creating *ecosystems*. The government should leverage assets available within India's vast economy, its human and physical capital, to achieve strategic national security objectives. A successful ecosystem acts as a force multiplier by amplifying the impact of government policies.

Education, Universities and National Security

Since the Second World War, national security has become synonymous with being at the frontiers of knowledge: nuclear technology, space technology, radar, cryptography, GPS and Internet are a few well-known cases. It is difficult to forecast where the next breakthroughs in technology may occur, and which of those may have a bearing on national security. The creation of the nuclear bomb and the security implications of the space race could never have been anticipated. These innovations were possible because the United States has a strong culture of research and innovation at its universities, built up over decades. This talent could be leveraged to solve national security problems when the need arose, but none of it could be planned.

More generally, being at the leading edge of the knowledge frontier has been a crucial aspect of national security over the course of history. A great power is defined by its ability to produce knowledge in all fields, rather than simply being a consumer of knowledge produced elsewhere. A strong knowledge-based society and economy will naturally support universities and firms that are at the frontiers of knowledge, which house specialists in every imaginable discipline. The defence and security establishment can tap into this pool of experts as the need arises.

For India to enhance its knowledge capacities, we will need modern multidisciplinary research universities that are the best of class and can attract the best talent worldwide in the natural and social sciences. Talent attracts talent, creating hubs of excellence, training the next generation of researchers and innovators. India has done quite poorly in the most significant measure of innovative research output: publication in peer-reviewed journals. India's share in the global publication authorship by country stands at 2 per cent today; the United States is at 21 per cent and China has reached 10 per cent in a matter of two decades.

Higher education in India today is in the concurrent list of the Constitution. The regulatory system for higher education is still not conducive for freedom, innovation and diversity. There are high entry barriers for the creation of good universities, local and foreign. Currently, no Indian university institution figures in lists of the leading

100 universities in the world. It takes many years for a university to establish itself as a thought leader and to build a reputation that will attract the best minds. The task ahead is a large one.

While creating a sensible regulatory structure for not-for-profit and private institutions, there is an urgent need to strengthen public universities. These universities need to be reformed on many dimensions: administration, finance, research capabilities, cultures of teaching and accountability. No world-class research ecosystem can be created without serious commitment of public funds, or public institutions. High-end research is a risk investment, and the market does not supply it easily.

A body similar to the National Science Foundation can be set up, where the government can prioritize thrust areas through transparent, competitive, peer-reviewed funding of proposals. But this body must internalize norms that promote genuine excellence and innovation. It must not be merely another bureaucracy controlling Indian science.

India needs to transform itself into a knowledge economy, for which it needs to build institutions that can deliver higher education and focus on the frontiers of research. A knowledge ecosystem approach is desirable, which includes public and private universities, funding agencies, channelling of government funds for research, funding from private sources and a culture of research with workshops, conferences and journals that attract the best minds worldwide.

The existing infrastructure of security-related knowledge (especially on matters pertaining to hard power) is deeply deficient. The gap between the government and the wider community of security studies remains large. Bridging this gap will require action along two lines. First, we need to foster more study and research in these areas. Institutions that were designed for these purposes have been unable to make much of an impact on our knowledge base. Reorienting them will also require addressing the quality of higher education in the areas of international relations and security studies.

The ultimate strength of the national security system will always depend on the human quality that populates the system. There is a dearth of human resources, in terms of both quantity and quality. While the former needs to be quickly made up, the latter requires educational platforms that impart skills required at various levels of the national security system. Most civil service officers are generalists and learn on the job. We need an educational and training structure that integrates civilian officers with the military counterparts. The Indian National Defence University must be speedily established.

We also need to increase the capacities of our training institutions to attract foreigners from friendly countries especially in our strategic neighbourhood. Presently, for example, we are unable to meet the demand from foreign countries for vacancies in institutions like the National Defence College (NDC) and the Defence Services Staff College. Conversely, we need to meet the demand especially from countries from our strategic neighbourhood and establish training teams in these countries.

Second, we need to consider ways in which we can leverage the available expertise for the government's requirements. To do so, we need to address the fundamental problem of information asymmetry between the government and those working outside. Those within the governmental system believe—with some justification—that they have something of an edge in knowledge pertaining to specific policy issues, and that there is little that outside experts can contribute to their functioning. Yet, this is a narrow view of the role of experts on policy issues. For, outside experts are required not so much to second-guess policymakers as to help them contextualize and conceptualize policy problems. Then again, we need to come up with ways of sharing classified information with outside experts to enable them to produce work that is attuned to the requirements of policymakers. We need to institutionalize a system whereby we contract specific pieces of policy-oriented research to domain experts, and grant them grades of clearance depending on their backgrounds and on the sensitivity of the work at hand. Such an arrangement will go some way in bridging the prevailing gap between information and expertise.

Strategic Communications

Strategic communications shape beliefs and influence behaviour. It is an important component of a nation's soft power. Good governance requires good strategic communications as one of its primary functions. Communications have strategic value based on the impact they create on the intended audience. The audience for communications in a democracy spans domestic and international spheres. The function of strategic communication in governance has increased in importance due to the IT revolution. This poses both opportunities and challenges for governance. The opportunities are centred on the fact that government's ability to communicate to the populace has increased substantially and will continue to do so. The challenges emanate from the fact that the populace will increasingly be exposed to communications that originate from diverse, non-official sources. These communications flow through multiple media that include print, Internet, audio-visual and word of mouth, each medium with several strands, like the Internet which has a plethora of streams, now referred to as the social media. Government has no choice but to have a presence everywhere in order to communicate effectively.

In a democracy, effective strategic communications is required between the executive, the judiciary, the legislature and the populace. It is also required for diplomatic, security and developmental purposes. Government policies must be communicated to the targeted audience with an understanding of their beliefs, motivations and interests. A communication plan must accompany the execution of policy. The plan must consider the targeted audience, the rationale for the communication, the means of dissemination and the feedback loop. In essence, planning, policy evolution and execution must consider the importance of communicative value and not only the mere physical impact.

India has to acknowledge the importance of communications as a function of governance. There is a need to nurture a strategic communications culture in government that privileges its importance and guides the execution of policy. But it must be stressed that internalizing the importance and value of communications is central to improving the effectiveness of governmental communications. Restructuring may be required. But an overarching architecture for governmental communications will not work, as in a democracy one cannot avoid the cacophony of opinions. Acknowledging the need and changing existing governmental strategic communications culture is the way forward.

Cyber Security and National Security

Cyber-security threats point to sophisticated attackers, some of which appear to have resources that can only be commanded by a state actor. There have been multiple instances of such threats, including Google's claims of China's hacking of Gmail and the breach of the NASDAQ Directors Desk service. Systems such as those of Google are well protected and defended, and employ the best computer security professionals worldwide. The IT systems that are at the heart of critical IT infrastructure institutions (CIIIs) are possibly much more vulnerable. CIIIs include both government and non-government institutions: various infrastructure conduits (power, air, railways, water and oil, telecommunications), banks, stock exchanges and depositories, health care, taxation, industrial applications and other government IT systems are vulnerable to attack. Many of these systems are complex, of systemic importance, and can have cascading effects, as demonstrated by the 1990 AT&T network crash and the north-eastern US blackout, almost two decades apart.

It is possible that such outages may be intentionally triggered by unfriendly state or non-state actors. Today, cyberattacks are powerful enough that the means of carrying out the attack can be classified as a weapon. Stuxnet may have set Iran's nuclear programme back by three years, which is what an air strike would have achieved. The very nature of the Internet makes it difficult to identify the source of the cyberattacks. Even today, it is difficult to identify the command and control centre of botnets, which are created by viruses infecting computers and installing back doors through which commands are executed.

It is thus not very surprising that the Department of Telecommunications has expressed concern over the use of Chinese telecommunications equipment in Indian networks. The US-China Economic and Security Review Commission in its annual reports note China's cyber activities and the impact on US national security. The United States has also set up a US-Cert and a Cyber Command whose mission includes 'conduct[ing] full spectrum military cyberspace operations in order to enable actions in all domains, ensure US/Allied freedom of action in cyberspace and deny the same to our adversaries'. Recently, a cyber-security policy was also announced by the US government with a comprehensive near-term action plan.

The following measures may be taken to strengthen cyber security (some of these were made in the report of the Technology Advisory Group for Unique Projects under the chairmanship of Nandan Nilekani). India should set up a cyber command with offensive and defensive capabilities. This body should also be responsible for setting domestic procedures to respond to such attacks, as well as developing capacity in the various CIIIs so that there is better system-wide knowledge of our capabilities and shortcomings. As mentioned earlier, for this to be successful an ecosystem approach is necessary, and security-specific skills need to be imparted at all levels. An entire industry revolving around cyber security needs to be developed, including student training, insurance, software security companies, and so on. All this responsibility will inevitably be decentralized, and cannot be met by a single central agency.

ICT in National Security

Information and communication technology and national security intersect at various points:

a. Cyber security: Critical IT infrastructure institutions need to be protected against external threats.

b. Data mining: Data from disparate sources (such as intelligence agencies, police, Financial Intelligence Unit, news, etc.) can be mined to extract intelligence and discover linkages.

c. Defence infrastructure: Software is at the heart of almost everything—aircraft, ships, vehicles, logistics, signals, command and control, and even the gear of the future soldier.

ICT has become a comparative advantage for India, although it did start out at the lower end of the spectrum. The problem is that much of the software is often imported with defence hardware, rather than being developed indigenously. The local prowess in ICT is a valuable asset that should be leveraged by the defence establishment. The volume of defence spending in India is large enough for dedicated firms to be set up just to serve the national security needs.

The key benefit to having a culture with highly innovative

firms (particularly start-ups) in multiple sectors is that they are able to attract talent and provide high-paying jobs. Such an environment is inherently highly competitive, and thus a good environment for defence contracting because of their increasing sophistication. This also helps build a highly skilled workforce which can be readily tapped to cater to the needs of national security. But domestic start-ups are not in and of themselves sufficient: foreign firms must also be allowed to set up operations in India.

Opening a business in India is particularly complicated because of problems with long registration times, access to credit and complex taxation. Even larger firms face problems with labour laws, contract enforcement, closing businesses and property rights. Foreign firms are challenged even further by capital controls and mandatory partnerships with local firms (in many sectors). Despite these challenges, domestic firms have become world leaders. Further simplifying the environment for doing business will lead to firms being set up to serve the national security requirements. These firms will draw on resources from the rest of the economy, while generating spillover effects for the rest of the economy.

Defence Industry

One factor constraining our hard power is the state of our defence R&D and defence production. This is a major strategic weakness that demands our immediate attention. India is supposedly a $100 billion arms purchase market, which is likely to surge to $120 billion in the next plan. The main challenge is to leverage India's burgeoning defence market to ensure progress towards greater defence industrial self-reliance. The choice we face is between techno-nationalism and techno-globalism. We need to move from techno-imitation to techno-innovation by unleashing the power of private industry and energizing state-owned defence industry institutions.

The nub of the problem at present is the near monopoly maintained by the Ministry of Defence through the Defence Research and Development Organization (DRDO), defence public sector undertakings and the Ordnance Factory Board over these areas. The absence of competition and the seeming availability of all governmental resources have hindered these research, design, development and production agencies' ability to innovate and deliver, and have instead mostly confined their activities to assembly-line capacity. The policies adopted by successive governments have prevented the

Indian private sector from unleashing its energies in this domain. These policies have also undermined attempts to form joint ventures with Indian and foreign firms. We need to urgently review and revise our current policies. An indigenous defence industry will be indispensable to the acquisition of credible hard power. The present system can at best absorb the existing level of technology but it cannot on its own develop the next generation. So, we keep going back to the need for transfer of technology, in an unending cycle of hope to meet our needs in this way. But the fact is that there are certain technologies which others are unlikely to give us, and so we also need to think creatively about enabling the DRDO to concentrate its expertise on developing technology that nobody will transfer to us. We should craft a defence technology strategy that combines global technology access with the creation of indigenous capability to innovate, coupled with an expansive subcontracting base.

The defence sector has historically had few linkages with the rest of the economy, but this pattern must change. For the volumes of procurement done by defence establishments, there can be large positive spillover effects into the rest of the economy. The Kelkar Committee report titled 'Strengthening Self-reliance in Defence Preparedness' has discussed some of these issues in more detail. The Indian corporate sector should be provided a level playing field to compete with government entities. This will require substantial policy changes in several areas including the taxation and export control regime.

India is poised to spend over $100 billion on defence procurement over the next five years, making it one of the world's largest buyers of defence equipment. This position of strength should be leveraged in procurement, driving strong competition among vendors. Historically, with large purchases, there has been technology transfer to set up indigenous manufacturing. Unfortunately, this has not transferred into new projects that continuously improve upon the state of the art. Much of the research continues to happen in public sector defence establishments, where performance and productivity are not transparent.

Much of the high-end procurement ends up happening from foreign countries, which benefits the economies and industries of those countries rather than India. There is always the lurking fear of malware in equipment procured from abroad. An indigenous ecosystem based in India, which designs and develops high-end products, is an ideal way to hedge such risks. Additionally, the use of open standards and open-source software as much as possible is another way to retain strategic control. The architecture of the Unique Identification Authority of India (UIDAI) demonstrates that large-scale mission-critical IT systems can be built with open-source software, thereby reducing external dependencies.

It is essential that an ecosystem that includes exports be created, which achieves these objectives as part of an integrated strategy for long-term national security. In particular, international purchases and their related offset policies should be used to kick-start a domestic ecosystem. A combination of this with an open procurement procedure should be enough to encourage a local defence industry. And one of the big advantages of this is that there is two-way spillover from such work. Military technologies can benefit from innovations in civilian technology and vice versa.

The Way Forward

Threats to national security can no longer be addressed by simply having more armed forces and buying more military hardware. National security is deeply and intricately linked to the knowledge society and the knowledge economy, which at its core is multidisciplinary and highly collaborative. An ecosystem approach will encourage collaboration within government, and make it possible to leverage the assets in the rest of the economy for achieving progress in education, research, technology, cyber security and defence production.

Today, government tends to operate in silos, and with hierarchical structures, with little collaboration across government agencies. We may note that the United States, until the 9/11 attacks, operated in a similar way. However, in the face of adversity, it reorganized itself to be much more collaborative. This was evident in the mission carried out in Abbottabad by Navy Seals with support from the Central Intelligence Agency and other intelligence agencies.

The transformation of governance to meet India's coming challenges will require an administration that is porous to ideas and people. Government will need to be able to draw talent and expertise from corporate firms, academia, think tanks, professional communities (lawyers, economists, accountants and project managers), NGOs and the media. Government must enable these diverse communities of knowledge and expertise to share information and ideas, and to work in collaborative ways, so that an end result is achieved where the whole is greater than the sum of its parts.

CHAPTER 7

State and Democracy

The strategic options of any state are determined by its capacity and internal legitimacy. The Indian state is, in many ways, enormously sophisticated and very complex. Indian democracy also has deep roots. But both are now at an important crossroads. Our ability to manoeuvre strategically will depend on how we navigate these crossroads.

The capacities of the Indian state are rising, giving it new opportunities to act. If India's economy can achieve growth rates of around 8 per cent a year on average for the next decade, it will lead to an unprecedented expansion of resources available to both the state and society at large. India has, by comparative standards, a relatively low tax to GDP ratio. This will rise with growth, with improved collection and deployment of technology and with new architectures like an integrated goods and services tax (GST). The GST will also help achieve one of India's strategic objectives in terms of domestic economic architecture: an integrated internal market. There must be a consensus on augmenting India's resource base. But resources are not likely to be as binding a constraint for the Indian state as they once were.

In many respects, these resources are already being redeployed to expand the state in crucial areas. A rights-based welfare state—that promises its citizens full nutrition, education, health and housing—is being constructed. If it can deliver these public goods adequately, there is no stopping India. Infrastructure too is being expanded. The state now has the capability of deploying technology to acquire the attributes of stateness: through the identification of its citizens. A combination of resources and technology presages a new era in Indian state building.

This is also a time when there is considerable experimentation with new institutions. A whole range of laws like the Right to Information Act, new practices like social audits, new performance contracts for state employees, the creation of new regulatory institutions, several initiatives at the state level to better deliver services, devolution and decentralization—all provide a unique opportunity to reconfigure the Indian state and enhance both capacity and legitimacy.

And yet, despite augmented resources, technology

and willingness to institutionally experiment, there is still considerable scepticism about whether the Indian state will be able to take full advantage of this unprecedented historical opportunity. Most citizens still find it difficult to access the state without feeling alienated and subject to unpredictable responses from the state and its agents. The delivery of crucial social services by the state is at best mixed. The perception that rent-seeking is high is creating an internal legitimacy crisis. And even where there is no rent-seeking, the procedures and protocols of decision-making are out of touch with the demands of the time. The state seems to be riddled with all kinds of perverse internal incentives that hinder decision-making. The identity of the state is driven more by adherence to archaic processes than concern with achieving outcomes.

Further, the Indian state is still searching for the most effective scale and size at which to operate. While much of the attention of economic reform focused on getting the state out of certain areas, there was much less attention to areas where the state needed to get in—to expand its presence. In crucial domains where the state needs to exercise its sovereign functions like law and order, justice and welfare, it is relatively understaffed or inadequately staffed. Even the quality of data available to the state to make informed decisions is under question because of the decline of its statistical services. State capacity should be understood in terms of both the quality of human resources and decision-making processes. Both need serious reconsideration and enhancement. These specific aspects of the state, more than anything else, are likely to be big factors that will hold India back and constrain its options.

There have been several proposals to reform the Indian state. Various reports of the Administrative Reforms Commission, reports on specific sectors like the police and numerous studies of accountability structures do provide useful material. Our brief discussion here claims to do no more than highlight one critical fact: that the accomplishment of India's strategic goals is bound up with the capacities of our state. We must ensure that these strategic goals do not founder because of any weakening of these capacities.

In fact, we need to dramatically strengthen these capacities. Reform of the state must be shaped by a clear sense of the knowledge architecture which modern states now depend upon. In the contemporary world this architecture must incorporate several features. First, knowledge is in a constant state of flux, so that states have to be nimble and able to move swiftly and effectively to grasp new knowledge domains and clusters. Second, given the speed of knowledge change and creation in today's world, it is inevitable that young minds, youthful researchers and practitioners, have a greater comparative advantage, and will be at the forefront of innovation and creativity. It is therefore vital that the state's decision-making structures and authority hierarchies should reflect this, and not remain wedded to hierarchical structures whose only rationale is bureaucratic stasis. It is also the case that knowledge innovation often occurs today by the combination of existing knowledge and expertise into new forms. This is particularly true of the kinds of knowledge that figure in strategic planning and decision-making.

Third, as we have seen in this book, virtually every fundamental strategic issue is interdisciplinary in its substance and requires the mobilization of different, cross-cutting skill sets. It follows that decision-making processes must have the ability to recognize and mobilize all appropriate skills, with a willingness to encourage unconventional combinations and conjunctions of knowledge domains. Fourth, it also follows that the design and reform of institutions must be focused by function and by solutions to the issues at hand; therefore the creation of knowledge and implementation teams must be problem led rather than constrained by institutional precedent and inertia.

Fifth, even as new and powerful knowledge forms emerge through connections across fields and by interdisciplinarity, we have also to recognize that we live in an era of hyper-specialization, even within disciplines: people within ostensibly the same fields are often quite unable to communicate with one another. Sixth, it follows that the burden of synthesizing and analysis is thus even greater: since the sources of knowledge are so diverse, government systems need to be devised that can break down the barriers between 'insiders' and 'outsiders' and allow constant turnover. The state must become more systematically open: porous both to expert knowledge and to those who can synthesize and interrelate what otherwise remain 'silo' domains.

The design of state institutions needs to assimilate these broad principles. This is especially true of the decision-making structures at the highest level: the Prime Minister's Office, Planning Commission and National Security Council. Their capacities to perform rigorous integrative and synthesis functions in the face of diverse knowledge fields and newly emerging challenges will need to be scaled up quickly and effectively.

These principles must also guide any reforms in the key security and intelligence agencies of the state: such as the Research and Analysis Wing, the Intelligence Bureau and the National Grid. The security domain also raises very specific practical and normative dilemmas, especially acute for a state like ours which rests on democratic legitimacy. The nature of security threats we face requires the state to accumulate evermore information; and technology has made it much easier to do so. But there are inevitable difficulties here: of informational overload, and of the ability of decision-makers to synthesize and draw actionable conclusions from the mass of information. Solving these problems will require careful design. At a normative level, the state's search for an accumulation of information and data about its citizens raises thorny questions about citizens' rights and civil liberties, and particularly about the increasingly sensitive domain of privacy. We cannot hope to address such basic issues merely by perfunctory discussion or by relying on supposed technical or administrative fixes. The questions at stake go to the heart of what it means to be an open and free society such as ours. It must therefore be a strategic goal to develop ways to give the state the necessary surveillance capacities, while preserving its legitimacy in the eyes of the citizens whose lives it aims to secure.

If the state is at a crossroads in terms of it resources, efficiency and capacity to make decisions, Indian democracy too is at a crossroads. Indian democracy has genuinely deepened on many dimensions: it has empowered hitherto marginalized groups, there is considerable institutional innovation, and the basic framework of electoral politics seems robust. But there is considerable disquiet that representative government is not translating into responsive government. This disquiet can be expected to grow—as a direct result of the success of Indian democracy. Aspirations are rising. As people become conscious of their own power they are less likely to put up with a state that does not respond. This can lead to critical face-offs which sap state authority and can in time escalate into a genuine legitimacy crisis.

As Indian society changes—in large part an effect of the workings of democracy over seven decades—so too the Indian state will need to adjust to these changes. It will have to devise different models of governance, in the face of a society that is becoming both better educated and more determined to participate in its government. One evident way in which governance models will need to change is in the recognition of a greater diversity and dispersion of power centres—that, after all, is precisely what a democratic society that empowers its citizens, as India has been doing, creates.

The traditional way of governing was founded on an asymmetry between state and society. The state could presume a fair degree of secrecy in its functioning. And the state often assumed that its actions would not be subject to detailed outside scrutiny: it believed in its own majesty. But recent legal instruments like the Right to Information Act, the explosive growth of India's media including the spread of new types of digital social media and a rising sense of self-confidence in civil society make the presumption of state opaqueness and secrecy untenable. Many of the current battles are expressions of these underlying shifts: where the state still operates by inherited patterns, and where society is increasingly impatient and resistant. The state must get ahead of these changes that society is pushing for; otherwise it risks being caught on the wrong foot. In fact, the best way for the state to increase its own strategic space for manoeuvre is to make its operations more transparent and open to citizens.

The second assumption of the inherited pattern of state governance was that power would remain hierarchically ordered not just within the state, but also in society as a whole. It would thus also define the state's relations to other centres of power in society. But in fact power is now deeply disaggregated across the Indian system, along many dimensions. It is disaggregated horizontally within the state, with different state institutions jostling for space. This can potentially be a source of strength in as much as it provides for checks and balances. Power is also disaggregated across society: political parties find it increasingly difficult to sustain steady support from the electorate, and across the country new forms of social movements and organizations are emerging that are crowding the political space once dominated by political parties. New arenas of governance are being created, which are redistributing power from the centre and state governments to more local structures of governance, while civil society itself is highly fluid, with social mobilization and centres of power emerging and subsiding with sometimes bewildering speed.

India will therefore need to build a new architecture of multilevel governance. Part of the reason the aggregation of relevant interests is becoming difficult is that the apportionment of powers between different levels of governance remains suboptimal. Power is too centralized in some respects; and where it is devolved, not enough capacity has been built to handle the appropriate functions. Many of India's conflicts, many of its state failures, can be traced to the inability to get right the distribution of powers and capacities that multilevel governance requires.

On the one hand, the disaggregation of power enables a vibrant, more inclusive democracy. On the other hand, the state will now have to function in a context where its authority will be challenged from many directions. This need not be debilitating. But it will require the creation of new institutional arenas of negotiation, where the emerging contenders for power and authority can engage and arrive at compromise and consensus. It will also require agencies of adjudication to decide disputes, whose legitimacy will rest on the capacity to project impartiality. Again, this sort of extensive institutional reconstruction and innovation will need considerable strategic will: to evolve protocols of negotiation that do justice to the complexity of interests, and above all to create and sustain impartial forms of authority which all contending parties can respect and by whose decisions they will abide. In this respect, the next generation challenge for Indian democracy will be to move forward from a view of legitimacy as simply based on electoral efficacy to a view of legitimacy based on impartiality: impartiality both in regard to the hearing of all interests and in their composition into workable consensus on matters of national interest.

It follows that how government functions will have to change in many ways. For a start, government will need to engage much more seriously with the media and with arenas of public debate. In its relation to the media, government has in recent times become overly reactive—following rather than leading, and apparently uninterested in conveying the finer points of policy, let alone setting the agenda for debate. Communications and continuous engagement with public opinion are not optional extras for modern governments: they are central to the successful pursuit of strategic goals by government.

Building consensus on long-term objectives and on national interests is of particular importance in devising an effective strategic vision of India's global opportunities. India will need more non-partisanship and more cooperation between the state, private business and civil society in navigating the unchartered waters of a very volatile international political and economic order. Our politics will have to evolve cultures of criticism, and of trust, where ruling parties and Opposition, state and private enterprise, take each other into confidence. The public assessment of policies must be considered in the context of long-term objectives, not short-term point scoring. It is vital that our public life sustain a critical culture: but criticism must be purposeful, not opportunist.

The need for political consensus is a cliché. But it is absolutely vital. There are bound to be disagreements. And many such disagreements can be strategically productive. They can be used as arguments to strengthen India's bargaining positions in international negotiations, and very often they help to arrive at sounder, more robust policy choices. But they can be debilitating as well. When our competitors know that the Government of India cannot deliver on promises, or has little room for manoeuvre, the nature of the bargaining changes. We must be wary of allowing our greatest strength, our democracy, to become an excuse for our dilatoriness and lack of focus.

Democracies elect leaders, and ultimately there can be no getting away from the fact that the political leadership has to take responsibility. In a democracy only a political leadership can have the authority to mobilize genuine consent. The administrative apparatus of the state takes its cues from the example of the political leadership. No amount of structural reform of the state, or continuous economic growth, will yield the necessary dividends if political leadership is indecisive, irresponsible or indifferent.

Conclusion

There is every reason to believe that, if India takes the right steps, it can assume its rightful place in the world. Its principal challenge remains lifting millions of impoverished citizens out of poverty. This should remain the litmus test for policy. There can be no compromises with this objective. When all is said and done, India's standing will be determined by how much it redeems this promise.

India has to remain conscious of the fact that it has a very long way to go in achieving this objective. But the last three decades have demonstrated that this goal is within India's grasp. High economic growth is possible. Creating structures that allow more and more citizens to participate in that growth is possible. India has unleashed among its citizens an aspiration and energy that is translating into the kind of dynamism not seen in Indian history for millennia. But much more needs to be done to take full advantage of this opportunity.

India has done all this while maintaining a commitment to a liberal, secular, constitutional democracy. India has held together as a nation because of a commitment to these values. India's strategic objectives will continue to be framed against the backdrop of both its development needs broadly understood and its constitutional principles.

But India has had a special history in one respect. Its nationalist movement was unique. It was unique in the techniques it deployed. It was unique in its intellectual ambition. All of India's great leaders—Gandhi, Tagore, Nehru, Ambedkar—had one aspiration: that India should be a site for an alternative universality. India's legitimacy today will come from its ability to stand for the highest human and universal values. These values gave India enormous moral and ideological capital. Except for our neighbours, with whom we have complicated ties of history, the rest of the world has looked upon India with a certain admiration for holding on to these values.

But as India ascends the world stage, the question will be asked: Will India be like great powers of the past? Or will it work to set new standards in moral and ideological leadership? In many ways the paradox is that precisely at the moment nations become powerful, they are vulnerable to being blindsided by their own ambition. Precisely at the moment they have an ability to shape the world, they shape it according to imperatives of power. India must remain true to its aspiration of creating a new and alternative universality.

In international relations, idealism not backed by power can be self-defeating. But equally, power not backed by the power of ideas can be blind. India's adherence to values will be a great source of legitimacy in the international system. It should, as it rises, be clear about what values it stands for. India already has enormous legitimacy because of the ideological legacies its nationalist movement bequeathed to it. But this legitimacy, if squandered, cannot be easily recovered. India should aim not just at being powerful: it should set new standards for what the powerful must do.